MY BROTHER BENJAMIN

26

"BEWARE!"

Words by H. W. Longfellow.

Music by E. B. Britten.

My Brother Benjamin

BETH BRITTEN

faber and faber

Dedicated to the memory of our father and mother
Robert and Edith Britten

This edition first published in 2013
by Faber and Faber Limited
Bloomsbury House,
74–77 Great Russell Street,
London WC1B 3DA

Typeset by Faber and Faber Ltd

Printed and bound by CPI Group (UK) Ltd, Croydon, CRO 4YY

A CIP record for this book
is available from the British Library

ISBN 978-0-571-29994-2

Contents

List of Illustrations

Preface to the 2013 Edition

There was not much money to spare in the dentist Robert Britten's family. He pawned his pocket watch several times in order to send his children to school. Yet the love, fun and generosity that pervaded the four Bs (their father's name for his children, Barbara, Bobby, Beth and Benjamin) must have been born of the happy, secure household in Lowestoft, thanks, not least, to their beloved Nanny and Alice the cook. In her book, my mother Beth relates their experiences of swimming in big seas. My siblings and I have strong childhood memories of them leaping, whoosh, into the water.

We adored our uncles and aunt. Robert and Ben were very funny, a fact not always known about my famous uncle. They had a wonderful aptitude for puns and were very charming, apparently just like their father. Benjamin was always very generous with time, help and money to many people, especially his two sisters. Beth had difficulties with finance after my father died in 1973, but her brother Ben stepped in and provided for her for the rest of her life, even long after his own death.

My very sociable mother had many friends. She founded the Over-60s Friendship Club in Otley, Suffolk, continuing to support them when she moved to Aldeburgh (where she lived for twenty-five years until her death). Every summer she invited them to her garden for tea and bingo and held a fête for Save the Children's Aldeburgh branch, of which she was secretary for many years. Sometimes she ran a competition to name the most species of the huge collection of plants in her wonderful garden, and she often revived friends' ailing plants with her green fingers. Many festival visitors and artists were welcomed to her bed and breakfast until she died just before her eightieth birthday. An ardent supporter of the Aldeburgh Festival, my mother was on the council until 1962, at which point she felt she should leave it to others more qualified than herself. She thought every concert there should contain a piece by her brother Ben, and stood up for him against all criticism. She could recognise his piano playing on radio or recording, especially his staccato.

It was a great sadness for her to leave her home in Otley on the break-up of her marriage, where she had created such a lovely garden and done so much work on the sixteenth-century house. With an eye for beauty and the ability to make it happen, she brought her creativity and artistry to her gardens, the dress-making for which she was trained, and later to uphol-stery and interior decoration.

Beth was a good mother to us three, and enjoyed her nine grandchil-dren. Her problem with alcohol made it at times difficult for her family and friends. Yet she was such a loving and good person that everyone returned even if she had been troublesome. She sought help after causing a car acci-dent when drunk, and her brother Ben paid for her two-year rehabilitation in Spelthorne St Mary, Surrey from 1971 to 1973. She recovered completely and after that only drank Coca Cola at parties. However, at her seventieth birthday party in 1979, friends said, 'Come on, Beth, just one to celebrate!' and although she knew she must not, she sadly gave in, and the alcoholism returned.

My mother had a hard time struggling through the Second World War. Perhaps it was this that led her to drink. She had also become a heavy smoker, encouraged by her father when she was eighteen. Her war years were filled with fear and worry. The Suffolk coast and Snape were in a dir-ect line for bombers aiming for London; my mother recalled hiding under the grand piano when they went over. With short rations, she had one, then two and three small children to care for while her doctor husband was of-ten away. Her brother Robert was a schoolmaster on the other side of the country, Ben was in the USA and her sister Barbara worked in London through the Blitz. (My aunt, too, was marked by anxiety for the rest of her life.) Ben's concern and love for his family is clear in his letters. My grand-mother Cuckoo (Dorothy Welford) adored her daughter-in-law's brother Ben. However, when he became a conscientious objector, she turned away from him, believing one should fight for one's country, as was her family's tradition. This was hard for my mother.

My parents' marriage was not a happy one; the difficulties began early on. My uncle Ben called it 'incompatibility'. Some time after the break-up Beth became deeply depressed, but the love of family and friends saw her through it, especially Ben's and Barbara's. Despite all the difficulties, my mother was overcome when my father died, so young at nearly sixty-three. Her brother Ben's death hit her extremely hard, also at only just sixty-three.

She had already started work on this book then, and he had said to her 'For Heaven's sake, get the facts right!' My mother admits in the book to being muddle-headed; many dates, places and other details in *My Brother Benjamin* were in fact inaccurate. However, I hope to have corrected everything in this new edition, and am very grateful to Richard Kelly and the staff of Faber Finds for re-publishing it, in time for the centenary of the birth of her wonderful genius brother Benjamin. My thanks also go to Beris Hudson and Ruth Donnocker who helped my mother with the original edition, my sister Roguey, my cousin John Britten and the staff of the Britten Archive at the Red House, Aldeburgh.

Because of her great devotion and admiration for her composer brother, Beth gave the royalties from her book to the Britten-Pears School for Advanced Musical Studies in Snape. The royalties from this new edition will also go to the school, now the Britten-Pears Young Artist Programme. I have sought to bring the book out again out of respect and love for my dear mother Beth.

Sally Welford-Lange-Schweizer
Forest Row, Sussex
November 2012

Acknowledgements

I would like to thank:

Roger Butler without whose help and encouragement this book would never have been published.

Elizabeth Sweeting who finally edited it, getting it into a good shape, and seeing that all details were correct.

Ruth Donnocker who researched the family tree, spending many hours in church vaults, county and town record offices up and down the country.

John Pudney whose programme notes I have used, I hope his family will forgive Arthur Oldham who allows me to use the article he wrote about the reception of *Peter Grimes'* first performance.

Joan Cross CBE who has given me her story of the production of *Peter Grimes.*

Bernard Richards who wrote for me the account of his first meeting with Ben outside the room where they were going to sit the entrance examination for the Royal College of Music.

Marie Slocombe MBE and Beris Hudson who did the typing for me.

Also the many friends of Ben and mine, too numerous to mention, who have contributed to the book by personal reminiscence, and I offer them my warmest thanks for this much appreciated help.

The author and her publishers wish to acknowledge with gratitude the generous collaboration of the Trustees of The Britten-Pears Foundation in permitting the use in this Memoir of letters, poems and drawings of Benjamin Britten, all of which are © The Britten-Pears Foundation, and are not to be further reproduced without written permission from the Foundation.

For the use of letters from Peter Pears, they are similarly indebted to the late Sir Peter and to the Executors of his estate; and they wish also to express their thanks to all the other copyright owners involved for consent to reproduce copyright materials.

The texts of the letters of Britten and Pears conform precisely to the original documents. Idiosyncracies of spelling and punctuation (especially conspicuous in the case of Britten's letters) have been preserved. There are no silent corrections.

Omissions are indicated by the following convention: [....].

The author extends her warm thanks to the staff of the Britten-Pears Library in Aldeburgh for their help in securing the exact transcription of the letters.

In this personal memoir the author has not attempted a complete annotation of her brother's letters. She points out that the complete and fully annotated texts will appear in *The Selected Letters of Benjamin Britten,* the first volume of which is in active preparation under the auspices of The Britten-Pears Foundation.

9th March 1987

Prologue

I went recently to Lowestoft to see the unveiling of the plaque which has been put on the wall by the front door of our old home, 21 Kirkley Cliff Road. It states simply: "Benjamin Britten 1913–1976, composer, pianist, conductor. Was born here on November 22nd 1913 and lived here for 21 years."

The house itself has changed very little, dental surgery is still practised there. I am sure the stair carpet is still the same and walking up those stairs, I could almost hear the piano being played. It was rarely quiet if either of my brothers was at home. The drawing room was upstairs on the first floor and in the summer, when the windows were wide open, there was usually an audience standing outside on the pavement listening.

My father's senior dental mechanic Ernest still works there part time. He told me that he made boats out of lead for Ben, to the envy of his school fellows; and was still doing the work that my father taught him all those years ago. He said that Mr. Britten was brilliant and much in advance of his time, especially in gold work. The roll top desk at which my father's secretary, "Lazy" Miss Hayes, sat, is still there.

Alas, the postcards which papered the nursery walls have gone, though they were still there when the room became Ben's bedroom until we left the house in 1934. It was Nanny's idea to paste all the picture postcards we received on the walls on wet days, when we could not go out walking.

I can see Ben now, walking past the house in the school crocodile, then gradually moving backwards, until as captain of school and captain of cricket at thirteen years old, he was walking at the rear with the master in charge, the pale blue colour-cap won for excelling at games, perched on his fair, unruly hair, which always stuck up however short it was cut. How he hated his hair; he spent hours trying to flatten it by much brushing. We horrid children teased him about it and told him he looked like the grocery assistant in the Home and Colonial Stores. When after his last operation his hair for a time went quite straight and he bemoaned the fact to me, I said: "But you always wanted straight hair", he said "I know, but I do not know how to arrange it." The waves came back a bit, but never as much as before.

What a joy he must have been to his parents, after three ordinary children to give birth to a Benjamin who excelled in all he did. How proud they were, how anxious too, to do the right thing for him; not to hold him back but also not to exploit his genius.

Aldeburgh, March 15th 1978

INTRODUCTION

The Family History and Background

We have very little evidence about our Britten ancestors, or about the other side of the family either, except those details which have been related from living memory. Our grandfather, Thomas Britten, lived from 1829 to 1883. By 1865 he had established a drapery business in Birkenhead, and in that year he married Charlotte Ginders, daughter of Jeremiah Ginders II and his wife Ellen Marsh. The Marshes, it seems, ranked as landed gentry and were opposed to this match on the grounds that Thomas Britten was socially inferior. He was, after all, "trade". It is just possible, however, that they may also have had better grounds for disapproval since the drapery business appears to have failed. When he died in 1883, leaving Charlotte with eight surviving children, the family was living in Maidenhead and he was running a dairy business. It was now that Charlotte revealed her character. Without financial aid of any kind – no widow's pension or child benefit then – she took over the business and set about building it up in order to provide for and educate her large family in the best fashion she could.

She was obviously ambitious for her children but two of them at least turned out disappointingly. The eldest son, Thomas, went into the army and was commissioned in the 7th Dragoon Guards, becoming a hard-living, hard-drinking young man. He went to the Boer War but died, unmarried, of delirium tremens on the way back to England in 1901. The youngest son, Edward, also proved to be a let-down. As a young man he went to Canada in some kind of cattle dealing capacity. While there he also married, in due course producing three sons and two daughters. But presumably his business operations were no great success because after a while he returned to England and, perhaps for want of any better aptitude, took over the family dairy business. But he was generally feckless and under him the business steadily declined. In the end, when his wife died, he was packed off to Canada, the family contributing to his fare, and his eldest son Edward went to Australia. The younger children were put into orphanages.

It was Robert, second youngest son of Thomas and Charlotte Britten, born in 1877, who was destined in due course to be father of Barbara, Robert, Ben and myself. He would dearly have liked to take up farming, but with no money in the family to set him up, he was sent to London as soon as he was old enough to be trained as a dental surgeon at Charing Cross Hospital. He hated this occupation all his life but, nevertheless, worked very hard at it and by degrees built up a highly successful practice.

The five daughters were all educated at a nearby dame school in Maidenhead, run by a Miss Hinton, and Florence, the eldest, actually went on to read History at Oxford. Subsequently she and two of her sisters, Julianne and Louise, set up their own private school for girls in Malvern. This was a fairly short-lived venture, closing down when Julianne married, after which Florence went off to Barbados as headmistress of the girls' high school, where she remained until her retirement in 1923. Julianne married the Rev. Sheldon Painter, whose family owned a prosperous drapery business in Malvern. The couple went to Japan as missionaries and stayed there for 27 years. Long afterwards my father asked her why she had never had children – she had once said she would like to have ten, all dressed in navy blue – "Sheldon never suggested it," she said. When they finally returned to England Uncle Sheldon was given the living of St Helen's in Worcester. The vicarage that went with this living was a lovely Georgian house in Cathedral Square where, as a girl, I loved to go and stay during the school holidays.

Aunt Julianne was the only one of the Britten sisters who had any kind of style: she had a natural flair for clothes and for making an attractive home. During one of my visits to them, when I was seventeen, I went out one morning to buy bread at a nearby bakery. One of the other customers in the shop was a tall, military-looking man with a white moustache, who seemed to be attracting special attention. After he had left someone asked who he was. "Sir Edward Elgar," was the reply.

Throughout our childhood the origins of our mother's family were even more obscure than those of the Brittens. In fact, there was a distinct element of mystery about them. One day I climbed up to reach the top of the bookshelves which lined one wall of our small morning room in Lowestoft where I knew there was a large family Bible. I had just opened this and was about to read the front sheet on which there were some written entries, when my mother came into the room and promptly took the book away from me. Sometime later I tried again when I saw it was back on the shelf, but now the front leaf was missing. Eventually I asked my mother why there was such mystery. She then told me that her father, William Henry

Hockey, had been illegitimate. He was born on the 1st May 1842 and his birth was registered in the sub-district of St Sidwell in Exeter. His mother was Fanny Hockey and he took her name because there was no named father.

Fanny, so the story went – was the daughter of a tenant farmer on an aristocratic estate and was seduced by one of the landowning family who was then unable or more likely perhaps, unwilling to marry her. Unfortunately I have never been able to find any clues which might identify the family in question, which is all the more a pity because it seems as if this might well be the source of the musical strain in the family. All the Brittens were completely unmusical, and there is nothing to suggest that Fanny's line was any more so.

In spite of her initial lapse Fanny afterwards married a sea captain and respectably produced several more children. Not surprisingly the eldest son William Henry's situation seems to have been an unhappy one and in later life he scarcely ever spoke of his family. He left home at 14 and went to live in London. However, by all accounts he was well educated and an accomplished musician, so it is possible that his unknown father may at least have provided for his education. He became a Queen's Messenger and the family lived in a flat at the Home Office in London, from which our parents were married in September 1901.

In July 1871, he married Rhoda Elizabeth Niblow, the daughter of a box maker, in St George's, Hanover Square, and scarcely a moment too soon, since their first son, William, was born the following November. Their second child, Edith Rhoda, was born on 9th December 1872. She was to be our mother.

At some stage William Henry took Rhoda to visit his mother who thought her not nearly good enough. "You are an aristocrat," she is alleged to have said, "and could marry anyone." She overlooked the fact that he was an aristocrat on the wrong side of the blanket. In their turn Rhoda's family omitted to mention that she drank, a defect that was to be a recurring problem throughout her married life. Sometimes when William called to see her during their courting days, he would be told she was indisposed, or had a headache and was lying down. Thereafter she had to be admitted periodically to a home for inebriates. Because of this and because one of her own brothers also took to the bottle later, my mother always dreaded that one of us would turn out to be alcoholic. For some reason she felt most apprehension about me and made me sign the pledge when I was fourteen – a commitment I have not always scrupulously observed.

There were seven children of the marriage. The four daughters were all sent to Miss Hinton's school in Maidenhead where they were contemporaries of the Britten sisters. Although they obviously knew each other, there is no evidence that any of the two sets of sisters were close friends except that eventually, presumably as a result of this link, the two families became connected. One of the Hockey sisters, Sarah Fanny – whom we knew as Aunt Queenie – later achieved some success as a painter, even exhibiting at the Royal Academy. Although her specialities were miniatures and flower pieces she also painted portraits of each of us children and her portrait of Ben as a boy is now in the National Portrait Gallery.

Musical talent displayed itself in another Hockey sister, Edith, my mother. She was an excellent pianist and as a mezzo-soprano she sang in the Bach Choir and often as a soloist in the Lowestoft choral society. All three Hockey brothers, however, were musicians. The eldest, William, became organist of the Tower Church in Ipswich and taught singing both there and in London until, in mid-career, he succumbed to drink, suffering what was termed "a nervous breakdown." Frederick, the youngest, was organist of Hadleigh Church in Suffolk up to the First World War when he was killed on the Somme in 1916. For many years afterwards my mother kept his bloodstained pocket book in a drawer, a relic which always held a macabre fascination for us children. Edgar, the middle one, went to sea at fourteen. Nothing was seen or heard of him for a long time. Then, late in life, he momentarily reappeared. Peter Pears was performing in a concert in Southend and came across Uncle Edgar, who was playing in the orchestra.

Because of their mother's drink-problem, much of the responsibility for running the family came increasingly to fall on Edith as the eldest daughter. When Robert Britten went to London as a dental student he began, no doubt because of the Maidenhead association, to court one of the younger Hockey sisters, the artist, Sarah. Then he switched to Edith, my Mother because – so he told my sister long afterwards – he felt sorry for her and wanted to get her away from her invidious situation. She was approaching twenty-nine with no obvious prospect of escape. So Robert and Edith were married in St John's, Smith Square on 5th September 1901, and in spite of this the marriage turned out to be thoroughly successful and happy. On the first morning of the honeymoon, Edith woke up to find no husband. She went sadly down to breakfast thinking Robert had left her. However he came in before she had finished. He had woken early and gone for a walk, she had not known his habit of early rising when on holiday. His younger son Benjamin was also an early riser, and a great walker.

The first of our family to settle in East Anglia was Uncle William Hockey and his wife Janie when he became organist in Ipswich. It was probably through this link that my father obtained his first post as assistant to a Mr Penraven, a dental surgeon in Fonnereau Road, Ipswich. Naturally, however, he was eager to be independent, so as soon as he could he rented a house in Marine Parade, Lowestoft, put up his plate, and in 1905, with money borrowed from his father-in-law, set up in practice on his own. Barbara, my elder sister, had been born in 1902; now came a son, Robert, in 1907, and I followed in 1909. Then there was a gap of nearly four and a half years, by which time mother was almost 41, before the last child was born – Benjamin.

These two letters from Edith Hockey to her father concern her life at Miss Hinton's School

Alexandra Road
Maidenhead
March 21st 1883

My dearest Papa

Today is Miss Hroyan's birthday. She has twenty presents altogether, some such pretty ones, some of us girls gave her a Green's History, she was very pleased with it. On the 16th, Miss Hinton's took place, we all collected and gave her a "Five o'clock Tea Service". She did have such a lot of presents, and such nice ones too.

Alice Room's sister came from Redhill to fetch her home this afternoon, her Mama was dying, and perhaps would not live until they got there. Poor little thing, I am very, very sorry indeed for her.

We have written to Edgar today as tomorrow is his birthday.

I do hope you are better. I was very pleased indeed to receive your nice letters and will try to profit by all you have said to me. I am going to try and pass 2nd Class College in June, also the Junior Trinity, but I will not say much as "Actions speak louder than Words".

I am so sorry you have lost your friend, and especially the shock the loss brought about.

With very much love and lots of kisses from
Your affectionate daughter

Edith Hockey

Alexandra House,
Maidenhead
May 23rd 1883

My dear Papa

It is Freddie's birthday on the 4th of June and we are making him a pair of socks and we have nearly finished them.

We have got a new duet and it is called "Sturm Marsch Gallop", so we have got two duets now.

Mrs. Hinton has set out her flowers and ours.

We have not heard from Mama yet.

It is Ada's birthday tomorrow.

Blanche had two mice and Ethel had one and they were such pretty little things and one night the cat had them.

I have not any more money and I owe Miss Belle fourpence.

We are going for a walk by the river this afternoon.

I send my love to you.

   Now I must say goodbye.

I remain your loving daughter.

Edith Hockey

P.S. Please may we have a penny each week.

From my aunt Queenie (Sarah Fanny):

Alexandra House,
Maidenhead.
May 25th 1883

My dear Papa,

Blanche and Ethel had three little tame mice and in the morning Edith went in the garden and she saw the kitten come out of the little house and she went and saw the cage door open and she took the straw out and the mice were not there.

   It was Ada's birthday yesterday and one of the young ladies told her to go to the cupboard to get a book and the pencase was for her and it has a piece of paper before it with Ada Hinton on it. Now I must say goodbye from your loving little Queenie.

On October 3rd 1883 my mother writes again:

My dear Papa

We have finished our socks and have sent them today with our letters I hope you will be pleased with them

We have a fresh boarder this term.

Mr Hinton came to see Mrs Hinton on Sunday week and when he went away he gave us sixpence each which we are going to buy a doll with.

Please Pa Miss Belle said I might ask you if we might have an umbrella between us as it so showery we get wet sometimes . . . . . .

We have written to Willie and sent him the pencil.

Now I must say goodbye.

I remain your loving daughter.

Edith.

1

Lowestoft

Lowestoft is the most easterly point in England. Although now the name is spelt with a "T" at the end, it should never be sounded. There have been many different spellings in the past, usually with a double "F" at the end. The town is ancient and now there is a harbour and it is a thriving port; there was no river in olden days. The cut through to the Broads, two miles away, is artificial; consequently there is usually a mud dredger near the mouth, keeping the way clear. Otherwise the opening would soon silt up.

In John Wesley's *Journal,* he speaks of the "Lowestoft Faithful". His first visits there were not happy ones. He noted that he had never seen a wilder congregation but that "the bridle was in their teeth", none behaving uncivilly to him at the finish. Other references speak of an affectionate people, of finding among them much life and love. It was his opinion that this town was by far the most comfortable of the whole circuit. Finally, before closing the Journal, he noted that at Lowestoft there was a "steady loving well-united society". It was strange, he added, that they neither increased nor decreased in number.

The reason that Wesley found much life and love was probably because the majority of the men were fishermen and constantly in danger. Also the fact that there was the problem of the ever-encroaching sea and the battle to keep it back. But they were very poor, also improvident. When the herring season was on they became suddenly rich and, being unused to having so much money, they spent it at once, often on expensive toys for their children. By the end of January the money had gone and then they went on relief. For most fishermen the herring season lasted from May, when they went to the North of Scotland with the drifters and followed the shoal south, to early December when the shoal disappeared, not to appear again until the following May, apart from a few longshore ones which hung about near the coast. The Ministry of Fishery Protection people were always trying to find out where they went. In spite of being poor, the locals were always ready to help anyone in need. How true is the saying "When in need go to the poor, not the rich!"

In 1914, when the Belgian refugees started to arrive after the Germans invaded their country, the townspeople could not do enough for them. Although I was only five at the time I can remember well going with Nanny and standing by the open bridge watching the boats go through crowded with women and children. They had not been able to bring anything with them. My mother had gone down earlier to help clothe and feed them and find places for them to go. Everyone in the town gave all they could. Even so, some of the women refugees grabbed what they could, hid it all and went back for more, though there was barely enough to go round.

The herring industry was the most important thing then, using all but one of the docks. Trawlers which caught flat fish were there as well, but not so numerous as the drifters, which were the herring boats. When the drifters arrived, so did the Scots girls, who followed the boats. The girls gutted the herrings and packed them in brine and barrels. For two months the town was packed with fisher-girls and fishermen, the girls, colourfully dressed in their bright scarves and shawls, walking about the town, knitting as they went. A strong smell of fish hung over the town.

My mother helped to run a canteen for the Scots girls in Whapload Road. When I was at home I helped there. We supplied them with tea and buns, for which they paid something, probably a penny. We could not understand a word they said, they spoke Gaelic, none of them spoke English. Next to the canteen was the first-aid room where their poor hands were dressed; the salt they used for packing the gutted herrings ate into their flesh. Even so, it did not stop them knitting. They must have been born with knitting needles in their hands.

It was amazing to watch the girls at work, both the gutters and the packers. They packed in enormous barrels, at the start disappearing from the hips up; then gradually they reappeared as the barrel became filled. They packed so beautifully and so rapidly. They were paid piecework. As it was November and dark early, they worked by the light of flares. I have never again seen such a sight: an area of two or three acres with hundreds of girls wrapped in their colourful scarves against the cold in that eerie light. I was quite frightened of walking there alone, it was a rough part of the town and there were a lot of drunks and nasty characters lurking. Sometimes Ben came to meet us if he were at home.

As a family we were enormously interested in the fishing. We had our favourite boats and knew all their names. Very few local people went near the fishmarkets, they despised them as being smelly, but we felt it was the most interesting part of the town.

And then there were the lifeboats. The Kentwell was the lifeboat at Lowestoft from 1905 until 1921. That was before the days of motor power, she had sails and oars only. When Lowestoft received her first motor lifeboat, the Agnes Cross, in 1922, the Kentwell was transferred to Gorleston. The tremendous advantage of the motor boat over sail and oars was realized in the rescue of the Newcastle steamer, the Hopelyn, on 19th October 1922. Her steering broke off the Norfolk coast and she was driven on to the North Scroby sands, where she was battered by a north-easterly gale with great seas breaking over her, and as the tide ebbed her back broke. The Caister lifeboat was launched but could not get off in the teeth of the nor'easter. Then the Kentwell from Gorleston was towed out of harbour by a tug but after a night of exposure could not get near enough to the Hopelyn to get off the men, who were by that time huddling in the tiny "Marconi room", as the rest of the ship was under water. The Kentwell returned to harbour, thinking there were no more men left on board to save, but soon after a distress signal was seen, so back the weary lifeboat crew went, but because of the enormous seas they still could not get near the wreck. Finally the Agnes Cross was called out and, because of the powerful motor fitted in her, she was able to get alongside and by degrees the unfortunate men on what was left of Hopelyn managed to leap and slither into the lifeboat, after an ordeal lasting for two days and nights.

All the men aboard the Kentwell and the Agnes Cross were awarded medals for their part in this dramatic rescue of twenty-four men and their pet cat. This is only one example of what went on at sea when we were children; we used to lie in bed and listen with fear to the sound of the gale roaring outside, and know that there were people in distress at sea. Many times there would be women and children drowned, for the owners of ships took their families with them up and down the coast; it was the only home they had.

There was of course no radar in those days and many fishing boats were lost and men drowned. The fishermen's wives were in constant fear of losing their husbands. If we had heard the rocket at night, we would go the next day to see the wreck, if it was near enough inland to be seen. Very often the boat would have been driven onto the beach, north or south of the harbour mouth, which was difficult to get into during a storm, on account of the sandbanks. Of course, the Lowestoft lifeboat was constantly called on during these disasters and some of the lifeboatmen were drowned as well.

There were always two or three tugs stationed in the harbour. These were used primarily for taking the smacks (sailing fishing boats) to sea on calm days. It was a wonderful thing to look out of the nursery window on a calm October day and see a fleet of smacks towed out to sea behind a tug. The largest, strongest tug was the *Lowestoft*. We were very proud when she was sent for sometimes to tow some of the big liners at Southampton Dock. There are no smacks at Lowestoft now; alas, for they were so beautiful with their great terracotta sails. But I am sure the fishermen must prefer their beautiful modern boats with all the creature comforts they provide and the equipment for their safety, such as radar and radio. Lowestoft now has a big shipbuilding industry, although it seems strange that they should build those factory ships for the Russians, who then come and take our fish.

When my parents first went to live in Lowestoft in 1905, they could walk along the cliff; a mile from where the cliff ends now, so much has the coast gone into the sea. Pakefield Church stands now near the cliff edge, whereas it was a long way off when first built.

If there was no wreck for us to go and see after a storm, we would go with our Nurse to see how many more houses had fallen off the cliff at Pakefield. This was the southerly part of the town of Lowestoft; we lived in Kirkley, the next area to the south of the town. After that there was country for three miles and then the village of Kessingland. The Borough of Lowestoft was protected from the sea, but between Kessingland and Kirkley it was the business of the County Council to keep the land from erosion. This they did not do; it was thought too expensive, as there was nothing but a few houses and fields to save. So we, thoughtless as children are, liked to go and see the damage done by the gales. Very often another house, or part of a house, had fallen and we could see half a staircase or even pictures still hanging on the walls, and could find treasures lying on the beach below the cliff, which is high at that point. The people who lived at the end of the row of houses which was most vulnerable – it ran east-west end on to the sea – were so loth to leave that, although warned to go by the authorities, they stayed on until the last minute, practically going over the edge with the house. The waves lashed with such fury at the base of the cliff that it was undermined. I, for one, never walk near the edge of a cliff; my memories are too strong to risk it.

The "rocks" at Pakefield, which we loved to play on, were not proper rocks at all, they were parts of the houses that had fallen into the sea. There was a wooden breakwater covered with seaweed. The bravest of us would dive off the end, the others go shrimping in the pools that formed between the "house rocks". There is lovely clean sand at Lowestoft and when the tide is out one can walk a long way, although it is not one of those places where the tide goes out so far that one can only swim at high tide.

The north end of the town was in a better position as regards coast erosion. An area called the "Denes" somewhat protected it. Even so the town built a great sea wall, with a road. During the last war, because the town was a naval base and everything on the coast was highly secret, the town authorities were not allowed to go to keep the wall in repair, although it had cost so much to build. We went to look at it after the war. It is impossible to believe what power the sea has until you see the evidence of it. Great chunks of concrete 20-feet square had been hurled into the air and landed some way away. The whole wall was completely destroyed.

The north end of the town, the old part, consisted of two roads running north and south, the High Street and the Lower Road. Between these there are cuttings, called "scores", which are narrow steps and slopes, and most of the fish smoking was done in these. The town was so badly bombed during the last war that some of them have gone, but there are several left. They have names such as Rant Score, Mariners' Score, Herring Fishery Score, Lighthouse Score, Martin's Score, Crown Score. All the Lower Road was occupied by the fishing: nets being dried, the fish auctioning hall, markets and so on.

The North and South parts of the town are completely separated by the river, over which the swing bridge joins them, whenever there is no shipping requiring to go up or down the river. This however happens frequently and very soon the land traffic builds up at this bottle neck. Recently a new bridge has been built but the situation is little better. It was always understood, if anyone happened to be late for anything, that it was to be blamed on the bridge being open. This of course was not always the case, but it was a good excuse. I remember on one occasion the organist of St John's Church, C. J. R. Coleman, was conducting a concert in the Sparrows' Nest. At the end of the first piece a large number of late comers filed in. Mr. Coleman waited while they took their places, then turned round and said: "The Bridge, Ladies and Gentlemen". There was a hoot of laughter. We were on the opposite side of the river from the railway station, so had to allow much more time for train catching.

The lighthouse stands guard on the cliff at the north end, sending a beam twenty-four miles out to sea. Next to this is a beautiful park "The Sparrows' Nest" where there is the concert hall; in our day it was open round the sides, with canvas awning which was put up in bad weather. We often went there to hear such famous artists as Mark Hambourg the pianist. Throughout the summer there were concert parties of varying excellence. Several times we went to the Olympian Gardens to see Nellie Wallace. She wore a "fur stole", which consisted of a length of string with a feather tied here and there, and she was one of the funniest people I have ever seen. We also saw Harry Tate with his crazy car and moustache.

The following is in a letter written to me in France by my father on August 19th 1928:

> Mum and Barbara are upstairs [our drawing room was upstairs] with your Aunt Queenie. The boys Robert and Beni have gone to the Sparrows' Nest to hear Mark Hamburg.

In summer Lowestoft shook off its drab winter garb and the place became full of visitors. We saw some very strange sights on the beach and walking round the town. It was not as it is now, when people, especially the young, are so smart in the latest fashion and in various stages of nakedness. I can remember as late as the early thirties, a special constable walked up and down the beaches telling men who were wearing only bathing trunks to put their tops on. In those days the women were often dressed in black satin and the men in their best suits, rolling up their trouser legs for paddling. Very few actually got into the water, people did not have the chance to learn to swim. We could always tell at what stage of their holiday they were by the degree of pinkness and rawness of their skins.

In the afternoons on the South Pier a military band played. We preferred the Grenadier Guards, for both Ben and I had a crush on the conductor and would dare each other to speak to him, as we followed him up the front afterwards. Sometimes he did stop and speak to us and asked us if we would like him to play anything special and, of course, we did ask for certain pieces. He looked so beautiful in his splendid uniform. We spent a lot of time, with Nanny of course, on the pier. On the beach there were also attractions, the chief among them being the Punch and Judy show, which we loved. There were also many religious groups. We thought the Church Army was the best value.

Lowestoft was considered to be a quiet respectable seaside resort and had no fun fair. For that we went to Yarmouth when we were older and could go on our own. Ben's chief delight was to go on the scenic railway. The Yarmouth one had come from the Wembley Exhibition and was very steep and, I thought, terrifying. However, Ben loved the feeling so much that he stood up going down the slopes to intensify the feeling of speed. I refused to go on with him, but we had friends with us who dared go with him, although he was always the only one who stood up going down. In the winter we went to Yarmouth to roller-skate on one of the piers.

At Christmas time there was always a family shopping expedition to Yarmouth, for the shops were larger and better than those in Lowestoft. Later I had a boy-friend whose father owned one of the Yarmouth shops. My mother was very odd about which families we should know, in trade. We were allowed to know my boy-friend's family, but we were not allowed to know the family of one of the big Lowestoft drapers. Perhaps this was because the Yarmouth family had a big house in the country, whereas the others lived in Lowestoft.

From our house we had a good view of the harbour and the shipping. To the north we could see as far as the eye could see, also straight ahead; but our vision to the south was blocked by a row of large houses. In the summer paddle steamers went daily from Yarmouth to Southend, calling at the Claremont pier in Lowestoft, packed with holiday makers. As children we watched the steamers from the nursery window, saying "Going, going, gone" when they finally disappeared behind the houses.

We also watched, and sometimes rode on, the donkeys going up and down our road in summer. They started at the preparatory school, South Lodge, at the bottom of the hill, and passed our house. We were always so sorry for them, the poor creatures, when they had to carry some very heavy people. The owner had a stick with a pin on the end to make them move when, as often, they refused to go.

2

The Family

First of all I must explain the reasons for the different spelling of my brother Benjamin's name. He was called Benjamin by my father and mother, hopeful that he would be the last child born to them. Naturally, Benjamin was a long name for a very small baby, so Benny he became at first. When he had learnt to write his own name, he decided to change the spelling to Beni. This lasted until he went to his public school and became Ben, which he remained all his life to almost everyone who knew him. The only people who ever called him Benji were Frank and Ethel Bridge, Marg Fass and Wystan Auden.

My sister Barbara was born in Ipswich on June 11th 1902. When she was three the family moved to 46 Marine Parade in Lowestoft, where on January 28th 1907 my brother Robert was born. Barbara was Edith after her mother and Barbara because they liked the name; all the family thought this most peculiar. Robert was Robert after his father and Harry after his mother's father, and Marsh, a Britten family name.

When baby Robert (known as Bobby to be different from his father) was six months old, on to this scene came Nanny, Anny Walker, from Farnham in Suffolk. My mother advertised for a children's nurse, and Nanny was at that time nurse to the Reverend Mr Bates's children at Blaxhall, near Farnham. She wished to get away from there; the under-gardener was pursuing her and she had no intention of walking out with him, much less marrying him. So she answered the advertisement and came to Lowestoft for an interview. My mother must have liked her, for she engaged her. She asked what wages she required, "£10 a year", she said. My mother thought that not enough, so she offered her £12, and Nanny became part of the family. For fourteen years she stayed with us, nursing us through our various childhood illnesses.

With the increase in the Britten family (we came along, although my father never intended to have children at all: there was no birth control at that time), the house in Marine Parade became too small and in 1908 the family moved to a much larger house up the hill further south, with a view of the sea and the harbour.

In this house, 21 Kirkley Cliff Road, my younger brother Benjamin and I were born. I came on June 10th 1909, one day before Barbara's birthday. Barbara, then aged seven was told she would have a lovely surprise on her birthday. When I arrived she was disgusted; she wanted a doll's pram, not a baby sister. Then, on a stormy night on November 22nd, 1913, by strange coincidence Saint Cecilia's Day, the patron saint of music, Bobby and I were asleep in bed. Bobby woke up at the strange noise he heard and called out: "Nanny, do go and pour some water on those cats". In fact, it was not cats but the first cries of his baby brother on entering the world. Barbara, who was sitting on the stairs outside the bedroom, waiting for the baby to be born, suddenly said: "Something wonderful has happened". "Yes, dear", said Nanny, "you have a new baby brother". "No", Barbara replied, "it is more than that". Ben insisted later that he remembered being born, he said he heard the sound of gas hissing. Since he always had such acute hearing, I suppose it is possible.

When my mother was carrying Barbara, Ben and me she had particular cravings and needed to do certain things. With Barbara she craved for oranges and to garden. Barbara loved gardening (but never liked oranges). With me she sewed. She was not normally a good seamstress, but did some good work then: she made the christening robe that Ben and I were christened in. And sewing has always been my chief thing. With Ben her craving was for music. She was a good musician anyway, and when pregnant she needed music all the time. It is an interesting question whether it was the unborn child directing her or her own need which influenced the child.

The morning after the birth – it was Sunday, so my father was not working – I went out with him in our car, a model T Ford. He was terribly proud of his new son and kept stopping and telling people he had another son, to be called Benjamin.

When Ben was three months old he got pneumonia. Nobody thought he could survive, but he did, probably due to the fact that my mother was breast-feeding him, as she did us all. She expressed the milk and fed him with a fountain pen filler, he was too weak to suck. She and Nanny "walked the boards" with him and he got better, although he was left with a weak heart, a "murmur" as the doctor said. The doctor told my father that he would never be able to lead a normal life, he must be treated with great care, cushioned from any sort of strain or effort. Fortunately our father's dental training was also medical and he had much common sense. He decided that would be a poor sort of life for Ben, and that as far as possible he should live as other boys. However, there were problems. He was a very sensitive delicate child and caught everything that was going around. I remember we had German measles together. I had it very mildly, while he was very ill with a high temperature and became delirious. I was fascinated because he kept talking about things crawling on the ceiling.

Ben always called himself "dear" when a baby. Out with Nanny in the pram, people stopped and looked at him, he was wonderful to look at. He had a mass of golden curls and blue eyes, and they would say "What a dear!", so he thought it was his name. After the war started, one day he was in his pram asleep in the garden. He woke up crying and when asked what was the matter he said "Bomb dropped on Dear's head". He talked very early and could only have been two at the time. The war started when he was nine months old.

As soon as Ben could walk he would go to the piano, scramble onto the piano stool and say "Dear pay pano". Until he was old enough to be up in the evenings, no one could have any music after he had gone to bed. Sometimes my mother or brother Bobby would try to play the piano very softly, hoping he would not hear, but he could hear and would cry as though his heart would break. This was hard on the family musicians but they gave in, because it upset "his lordship" too much. On the whole, and considering his delicate health, our parents treated him the same as us. Our father was always strict with his sons and taught them from an early age to be considerate to others.

After Ben was born, my mother felt she needed more domestic staff, so Nanny's sister Alice came to us as cook. We were all devoted to her, she stayed with us for eighteen years. She ruled the kitchen with a rod of iron, just as Nanny held sway over the nursery. These sisters were completely different. Nanny was adventurous and gay, and lived in a world of fantasy. Her father, we discovered afterwards, was a platelayer on the Great Eastern Railway, although she implied to us that he was Station Master at Liverpool Street. Her parents lived in a cottage right on the main road at Farnham near Saxmundham, not even a small garden in front. We understood that they lived in a house with a longish drive lined with trees. I remember when we first saw the cottage, when my father drove her home for a holiday, we were astonished and looked to see if she minded that we had seen the place as it really was. She didn't seem to mind at all. It was like that with her followers. One of them was a driver on the trams, dr. Thomas. She let us think that the "dr." stood for doctor. Our lives with her were consequently full of excitement. We didn't just go for a walk; wherever we went it would be somewhere interesting. Although, if she wished to be particularly annoying and we asked "Where are we going today?", she would say "There and back to see how far it is". Or if we said "How are we going?" – sometimes we went for a short way on a tram or in the car with Daddy – she replied "On Shanks' pony", which we, of course, found absolutely infuriating.

She was completely reliable and my mother could trust her absolutely with us. Nanny had a natural gift with all young. After she had to leave us and go home to look after her mother, she was involved with all the local families, whose mothers were only too happy to leave their children in Nanny's capable hands.

Alice was gentle in contrast to Nanny's tomboyishness. She never gave Nanny away when she was having her flights of fancy, but just smiled sweetly and the kitchen was the place where we all loved to go.

Although Nanny was reliable and good with the children, she nearly drove my mother mad with her untidiness. After the children were in bed, Nanny went down to the kitchen to have her supper with Alice and the other maids; after that she was supposed to go upstairs again and tidy the nursery and lay the fire ready for the morning. My parents related later to us that there would be dead silence for a long time, the nursery being over the drawing room where they would be and could hear everything. Suddenly about ten o'clock there was a lot of noise, the fire irons rattled, furniture moved about and general disturbance. Nanny had been deep in one of her beloved books, with a good fire and her feet on the fire guard. They let this pass, realizing that she must have time to relax after having been with the children all day.

Nanny and Alice finished their lives together, side by side in two little cottages on the main A12 road in Stratford St. Andrew, Suffolk. Nanny finally succumbed to the advances of Mr. Scarce, the man she had come to Lowestoft to get away from twenty-five years earlier. Alice married Mr. Pratt, to whom she had been promised nearly all the time she had been with us. They were unable to marry before, as Mr. Pratt's aunt was keeping house for him and they could not turn her away and did not want to share the cottage with her. We all knew about her "bottom drawer" and always gave her presents for it at Christmas and birthdays. It must have been full up by the time she left us in 1934 and got married.

We continued to visit them constantly when we grew up. Alice died first, and then the two husbands, so Nanny was left on her own. Crippled as she was, we were worried about her. There was no sanitation in the cottage except a cold water tap. No sink, no drains, only a dirt closet at the bottom of the garden. I went to beg the landlord to do something about it but he was so miserly he would do nothing, although we said she could pay more rent if he would put in sanitation. Ben suggested we might try to buy the cottage, but of course the landlord asked a ridiculous sum, having an idea who was the would-be purchaser. Ben, generous as usual, bought a shed with an Elsan toilet, which was put just outside the back door, where Nanny could keep her firewood dry and keep dry herself on wet days.

On Nanny's ninety-first birthday, I drove her to see her beloved Ben. Then, in the early part of 1974, just before she died, and when Ben was already very ill, I drove him to tea with her in her cottage. It was January and a gale was blowing. We were staying at his cottage near Diss, about an hour's journey away, and I was reluctant to take him, but he insisted as he knew that Nanny was expecting us.

After she died I suggested to Ben that it would be a rather nice idea to have a little memorial to Nanny. He agreed and I rounded up all the children she had looked after; they all wanted to do something in her memory. Finally we decided to make a gift to her church in Stratford-Saint-Andrew. It was a poor church and there was no proper chalice, so we gave a pair with the names of all her "children" engraved on them. There was a little ceremony taken by her first baby, Canon Naunton Bates, who has now retired to Blaxhall where he once was Rector. Benjamin was too ill to go, so his nurse Rita Thomson came instead.

3

World War One 1914–1918

During both world wars Lowestoft was very much in the front line and became a naval base. In the first war the attack started with Zeppelin raids. I shall never forget seeing one come blazing down into the sea and several others came down near us. On June 17th 1917 one came down at Theberton, a village 15 miles away. The blaze lit up the sky to such an extent that my father was convinced it must only be two or three miles from us, so he got out the car to go and see the wreck. He drove on and on until he reached Theberton. What was left of the unfortunate crew was buried in the Churchyard at Theberton. Ten years ago the remains were taken back to Germany, but there is a white wood plank showing where they were buried. The Zeppelin crews were all volunteers, there was no chance of their getting back alive.

Usually we were taken with Nanny each year to a farm at Capel St Andrew, a village some forty miles south of Lowestoft, near the coast where Nanny's uncle was tenant farmer. We stayed there while our parents went abroad for their holidays, mostly to Arosa in Switzerland or to Italy. During the war they had to stay in England, and were worried about our being so near the coast in Capel, so in 1915 we went to another farm at Newbourne, only two or three miles inland. The first night we arrived a Zeppelin came over and we all rushed outside to see it as it went on inland, probably to Ipswich. The next year we returned to Capel which we liked much better.

Although Ben was very young during the war, he was aware of all that was going on round him. Because of this my father was worried about keeping us all in such a dangerous place, but decided that it was better that we should all stay together, as he had to be in Lowestoft anyway for his work. So he had the cellar of the house fortified and made comfortable with chairs and warm clothes and emergency rations. There was water down there, as it was the place where the washing was done on Mondays. The water was heated in an enormous copper with a wood fire underneath. I suppose this fire was lit to keep the place warm when we were sheltering during raids; there was no other heating down there and I do not remember being cold, nor being frightened either. We just thought it tremendous fun to be got out of bed and taken down to the cellar and given cocoa and biscuits. Ben was carried down wrapped up in an eiderdown – his curly head sticking out at the top. An axe and spades were kept down there to dig us out if necessary.

Barbara was at boarding school in Staffordshire, to get her away from danger and Robert was at prep school in Forncett in Norfolk. Poor Barbara, first she had been sent to a school in Norwich as a weekly boarder, but she cried so much each Monday morning when she had to return to school that our parents could not stand the strain. As some friends of theirs were sending their elder daughter to Abbots Bromley they decided to send Barbara as well. Both girls wrote home of the horrible conditions and told their parents they did not get enough to eat. The friends believed their daughter and took her away, but Barbara was made to stay although she wrote home and threatened to run away to some relations who lived in Stafford. All this cannot have done her any good. She was and always has been a very nervous person.

We were all at home for the bombardment which happened in the early hours of April 25th 1916. We were all hustled down to the cellar, then Nanny marshalled the maids and shot upstairs to see what was going on outside. Pop told us afterwards that he had trouble making her stay in the cellar. She would keep rushing upstairs and hanging out of the windows to see the fun.

Lowestoft was very unprotected at that time; the Fleet was up north in Scapa Flow and there were two fishery protection ships stationed there then, the Halcyon and the Dryad. The Halcyon was at sea when the German fleet arrived. The story afterwards was that she was in such a hurry to get home that she jumped the sand bank. The Germans took advantage of the fact that the main fleet was away; they did not know that there was a small fleet left at Harwich. Fortunately for us, the shells mostly went over us to the back of the town, although one fell in the field opposite the house and a large piece went into the wall under the dining room window. By a miracle the windows were not broken. The crater from the shell was enormous. There was only this piece of rough land between us and the sea. The town suffered much damage but fortunately not many casualties. One shell went right through a row of houses without exploding and landed on a feather bed. Strange things happen at times like these. At one moment there was a sound of breaking glass and everyone thought the conservatory had gone, but it was completely intact when they were able to investigate. The shelling had gone on for some time before the small fleet from Harwich arrived. The moment the Germans saw the ships they fled, with our tiny fleet after them. By this time it was getting light, so we all came up from the cellar and were allowed to go to the gate and see the German ships disappearing into the distance.

After the bombardment of Lowestoft the powers that be decided that the town must be protected. So a Monitor was sent, called the Havelock. It was an enormous unwieldy thing; it could not go under its own steam, so had to be brought by six tugs and was manoeuvred into the harbour with difficulty. Of course, this was a red letter day for all the family. The town turned out in force to watch her come in and we all went, Ben in his pram for, although he was two and a half, he was not allowed to walk too far on account of his heart condition. Everyone felt that this monster with its huge guns did more damage than an air raid. If there was to be a gun practice, the town people were warned to open all their windows in case they would break, which in some cases happened. However we had no more bombardments. Perhaps she was a deterrent.

In a family of four it happens that there is a division into pairs. When we were small Barbara stood up for Benny. Being so much older, she protected him against the middle ones, Bobby and me. In those days we usually did things together with only two years between us, although we fought constantly. It was probably a good thing that Ben had a family, he could so easily have become spoilt and conceited.

As well as being so gifted – he was already playing the piano well and composing little pieces by the time he was five, and he wrote notes before he wrote words – he was also gorgeous to look at and all the ladies fell for him even then. I used to get so bored having to go out with him to tea parties given by his admirers.

My mother taught us all to read and write before we went in turn at the age of seven, to the two Miss Astles' dame school up the road. We learnt at home from a book called *Reading without Tears* with pictures at the top of each page. On one page there was a picture of a horse but underneath it said "Nag", so of course as each child came to this they said "NAG – horse". In spite of this funny book we could all read and write pretty fluently when we went to school. Fortunately the ladies Miss Astle and Miss Ethel were very good teachers. They took children from six to eighteen. In our case the girls stayed until thirteen and the boys until they were nine and went to the local preparatory school, South Lodge.

Miss Ethel was the music teacher. She taught by the Sepping system, done with several strips of wood supposed to represent the lines and staves of a sheet of music paper. We had to put the notes on them to make music. I wonder if it helped Ben, who was already composing by then. I enjoyed putting out the notes, but it did not make a musician of me. I struggled on for ten years, but my piano playing was a great joke in the family, my party piece was *The Carnival of Venice,* which I continued to play in spite of the jeers from my brothers. Ben was kind about it though and at one stage tried to teach me to play the violin, but gave it up as hopeless even though he did once tell me that, apart from himself, I was the most musical in the family.

Ben could probably have been a sportsman, a mathematician, a pianist, if he had not chosen to be first and foremost a composer. One day at a tennis party someone asked him what he was going to be when he grew up. "A composer" he replied. "Yes, but what else?". Ben excelled at everything he did and his school reports were always very good. Apart from all these gifts, he had great charm of manner, which he no doubt inherited from our father, who had many admirers. My poor mother, always conscious of being five years older than he, suffered agonies of jealousy, although as far as I know there was only one occasion on which she need have been worried.

One of my father's secretaries was determined to capture him and with all her female wiles did her best, but this was thwarted by Nanny who realized what she was up to. One day the secretary had gone home and on purpose had taken the keys of the desk with her, being sure that my father would have to go round and fetch them from her. Nanny fortunately found out what she had done and went herself to get the keys. After this the secretary was sacked.

My mother chose the next secretary. She was very plain, but she became part of our lives, as Alice and Nanny were. Her name was Miss Hayes; I suppose she had a Christian name, but we never knew it. Ben was about three when she came and he could not say his "s's", so he called her "Milhale". Then, she became known, quite undeservedly, as "Lazy", which she remained for the eighteen years she stayed with us. Lazy was a good and loyal friend to all of us. After her aged mother died and she left the practice she went to live with her sister in Kettering where we went to see her when we could.

Only recently did Nanny disclose the story of the secretary episode. None of us had any idea of it and we always knew we had a secure home and loving parents. My mother once said to me "Beware of the green-eyed goddess" – meaning jealousy.

4

Nursery Theatricals

Nanny had the idea that we should do plays to be performed at Chistmas to friends and relations. My parents thought it a good idea and had a rail put across the nursery so that a curtain could be hung to form a stage. We did many of the nursery rhymes. As there were only four of us and a large age gap, eleven years between Barbara and Ben, we all had to play many parts. When the two eldest, Barbara and Bobby, were away at school, Nanny copied out and sent the parts for them to learn, so they could be word perfect and ready for rehearsals on their return. One year she wrote to Bobby and said "This year we will do "Tabloids" instead of a play". Of course, she meant to say "Tableaux".

I remember when Ben was only three years old that we were doing *Cinderella*. He took two parts: one of the Ugly Sisters, and the page. As he tried the slipper on the other Ugly Sister, he said very quietly "I link it is a tifle mall". He had difficulty with S, as I said before, and R. "Say it louder", he was told. "I link it is a tifle mall" he shouted, as he gave the slipper a shove onto his brother's large foot. It must have been very funny to watch. I have memories of Alice sitting in the front row with tears streaming down her face. Alice always cried when she laughed.

The audience always dressed up for the performance, my father in tails with his top hat. He was his usual teasing self and kept pretending to look round the curtain. Nanny made and organized all the clothes herself and during the performance was very busy with her mouth full of pins and the prompt book.

We normally rehearsed on wet afternoons when we could not go for a walk, or after tea. If Pop was not too busy in the surgery he used to come up while we were having tea. Knowing what was going on, he tactfully made a lot of noise coming up the stairs and there would be a sound of scuffling while everything was put away.

In the nursery there was a rocking horse, bought about 1909. Our delight was to ride it so hard that we could move the horse across the nursery floor, which brought our father running up from the surgery, thinking we would bring the ceiling down. This same horse was in the first performances of Ben's opera, *The Little Sweep*. In fact it was used until the weight of carrying the entire cast of children on its back in the final *The Coaching Song*, was causing it to disintegrate. Having been repaired, the horse was returned to the family, where it has been handed on in turn to children of suitable age.

There was a hole in the horse where the pommel, used by ladies when riding side saddle, was supposed to be. We used to feed the horse with lumps of sugar or anything small that we could put in this hole. My father put a stop to this when he found out what we were doing, and filled the hole with plaster of paris. To this day one can hear the objects inside rattling.

Usually Nanny would be reading one of her penny dreadfuls and Ben covering his face with strawberry jam – he was very partial to this and called it "Billa", and we called him "Jammy Face" or "Benjammy". Suddenly, footsteps on the stairs: away would go the book into the capacious front of Nanny's apron. "Benny, wipe your face. Beff dear, don't tiptilt your chair, Bobby come to the table." All in order again before the door opened and our parent entered.

Apart from the Christmas plays, the family were involved in plays and pantomimes with their friends, mostly acted for charities. One of the most loved charities was The League of Pity, a branch of the NSPCC. A performance of *The Water Babies* by Charles Kingsley was given in the Sparrow's Nest. Ben played the part of Tom, dressed in skin-coloured tights with tiny fins sewn to his shoulders and heels. Mother played the part of Mrs Do-as-you-would-be-done-by. Although Ben's friends and my friends took part as water-babies, I was not allowed to be in it because I was too tall. I was very hurt by this, for I was the same age as the other girls.

At this time, 1919, when Ben was six, he started writing plays himself and acted them with his friends in the nursery. Most of them were about the Royal Family, because he was very keen on them, especially the young Prince John, who died. Our Aunt Flo was Headmistress of the Girls' High School in Barbados and met the Prince of Wales when he visited the West Indies. Ben wrote a play about that, an excerpt of which follows:

SCEN 3
P/W (PRINCE OF WALES)   WHY MISS BRITTEN
M/B [MISS BRITTEN]   YES PRINCE I AM MISS BRITTEN
P/W [PRINCE OF WALES]   GOODBYE MISS BRITTEN
EXIT MISS BRITTEN

SCEN 4
ON THE WAY FROM BARBADOES

LT [LIEUTENANT]   WELL PRINCE ARE YOU READY TO-BE DUCKED

P/W   WHAT ME BE DUCKED

L/T   YES ME DEAR PRINCE AND YOUR BROTHER TOO

P/W   OH NOT MY BROTHER

SCEN 5
ON THE WAY TO BARBADOES

L/T   NOW TO BE DUCKED. YOU TO. ALBERT

P/W   NO

P/A [ALBERT]   NOT ME OR YOU

P/W   NO YOU ARE NOT GOING TO DUCK ALBERT

L/T   YES I AM

P/W   <u>NO YOU AR'NT</u>

SCEN 6
ROYAL TRAIN

P/W   OH YES IM GOING BY THIS TRAIN ALBERT TOO.

S/M [STATION MASTER]   PORTOR PORTOR HERE COMES THE ROYAL PARTY. BE READY TO STAND ATENTION

P [PORTER]   PUFF, PUFF, PUFF, HOW THE TRUMPETS BLOW

MAKE UP

P/W he SHOULD HAVE A BLUE SAILOR SUIT AND LONG TROUSERS IN SCEN 1234 AND 5 AND 6 he SHOULD HAVE A TWEED SUIT. AND P/A SHOULD HAVE A BLUE ONE TO PS/M SHOULD HAVE A CADRBOARD CROWN, KING IN A RED DRESS QUEEN IN A BLUE DRESS AND A CADRBOARD CROWN.

THE END

Ben probably got the idea of the ducking from the stories Aunt Flo told us about what went on on board ship, and ducking of the princes appealed to him.

He also wrote poems about this time, some of which I still have:

POEMS
by
Benjamin Britten
"POOR WEE PUSSIE CAT!

Poor wee pussie cat!
Oh! a matter of fact,
you're much nicer
than all the mice er!!!

Ugh! how beastly they look
much nastier than the corn they took!
Poor wee pussie cat!
that's the matter of fact!!!

"THAT BAT"
What's that thing you're looking at?
What's that thing! oh it's a bat.
It's so funny for one to be here
It's trying to get my father's beer.

See it fly to and fro,
oh I do wish it would go!
It's worrying me, t'wont let me sleep,
oh do *let* me have a peep!

"UNHAPPINESS"
Oh I moan and I do groan!
I do groan and I do moan!
I try to be happy but never succeed,
till I look at some grass and call it a reed.

"THE BALLOON"
I look at the sky
and see it does fly,
oh my balloon! I love it
to see the sun above it.

"MY KITTEN"

My kitten is a pretty thing
It loves it when my mummy does sing,
also my sister, brother and father
it likes it when they sing er – rather!

"GHOSTS"

Ghosts, ghosts, did you mention a ghost?
Ghosts, ghosts, they boast, boast.
When you roast, roast, then comes a ghost,
then comes a ghost when you roast, roast.

5

Childhood

When Ben was seven or eight he started to go and stay alone with the Hockey family in Ipswich. It was thought that Uncle Willie could help him with music and Ben liked going there not only for the music but also because it was fairly near the main railway station, the Great Eastern. At that time he had a passion for steam trains which continued to a lesser degree in later life. Woe betide us if on our return from a train journey we did not know the train number, class, number of wheels, etc. However tired we were we had to go to the engine, and write down all these details. My cousin Elsie Hockey reports that sometimes she was told to take the small boy for a walk, she was eighteen or nineteen at the time; one day she was out walking with him and a girl friend of hers; they were near the Westerfield train crossing when suddenly Ben shouted "Run"; he had heard a train coming. They puffed and panted, but he got there in time to see the London train come through. Another day her mother, Aunt Janie, took him out. When they returned cousin Elsie asked her where they had been. "We spent the afternoon on Ipswich Station", she replied. "All the afternoon?" said Elsie in horror. "Yes", said her mother, "it was interesting. While we were sitting there watching the trains the Royal train came through from Sandringham loaded with flowers for Princess Mary's wedding to the Earl of Harewood". They little thought that Ben would be such friends with that family later.

Ben was very fond of his Uncle Willie and when I told him only a few years ago that Elsie had a difficulty finding her parents' grave when she visited the Ipswich cemetery to take flowers, as there was no money for a stone, he immediately said he would pay for one. My parents were both dead by the time the Hockeys died or they would have seen to it. It was typical of him to think of others, and even before he himself was well-off, one only had to mention that someone needed help, and if he possibly could he would give something.

When Ben was very little he did beautiful drawings, very detailed and expressive; and everyone thought he would be an artist. Even when he was only three the detail in these tiny drawings was extraordinary. The one shown here was drawn for my autograph book when he was six or seven.

Nanny left when Ben was eight years old, and Barbara nineteen. Although my mother was sad to see her go, she felt it was right, for young Ben was having things too much his own way. For instance, when he was bathing, he would be reading a book, while Nanny washed him: "Lift your leg, dear; now the other one. Now get out and I will dry you", Ben meantime deep in whatever he was reading. If nothing else came to hand he would read a railway time table, he read everything he could get hold of. It was understandable that Nanny should spoil him. But she did not spoil us. When a child, I did not sleep so well and had horrid nightmares. I knew Nanny would not come on demand. She had had us all day and was probably tired. So, if I felt I wanted comforting, I waited until I heard her go downstairs for her supper and then yelled for Mummy who never failed to come whatever she was doing.

People have asked from time to time if we were ever jealous of our little brother but I can honestly say we were never jealous at any time during our lives, although certainly we were proud. Bobby might well have been jealous, for he also played the piano and the violin, but Ben far excelled him from an early age. Ben was wicked too, for if Bobby was playing something on the piano that Ben did not like he would tell Mum that "he had a thought", which meant that he wished to compose. Mum was always taken in, although we were not, and told her so, feeling it was not fair to stop Bobby playing. Usually Bobby played ragtime or light music, so the result was amicable and they each kept to their own thing. Then one day naughty Ben decided that he would have a go at ragtime and of course he played it much better. There was quite often rivalry between the brothers in spite of the seven year difference in age.

The arguments over the piano became so acute that my mother decided she must get another one. At that moment, a friend of hers, Mrs Doveton Boyd, had just lost her husband and was moving with her daughter Elizabeth – a girl friend of Ben's – to a smaller house and could not take her square piano, so she lent it to us. It was put up in the boys' bedroom, the old nursery. In the summer when the windows were open, a crowd of people used to collect outside on the pavement to listen to the music which poured out of the house.

Our cousins and relations delighted in calling us the four B's. We found this very tiresome, especially when letters came addressed to Miss B. Britten or Master B. Britten. In any case only two of us were really "B"s, Barbara and Benjamin.

Although we quarrelled and fought frequently we were a very united family and very fond of each other. There was always a lot of laughter. My father was a very humorous man with a good sense of the ridiculous and so had we all. I thought my big sister bossy and tiresome sometimes and she was always saying such things as "When I was your age I wasn't allowed to do such and such.", but if anyone hurt her I was the first to defend her.

When Bobby was fourteen and due to go to Oakham School, he developed sleepy sickness – encephalitis lethargica. There was an epidemic at that time, although how he got it was a mystery; some doctors thought there might be a connection with the fact that he had just been vaccinated for the second time, at the insistence of the school, having been done as a baby. Nanny, who had gone home to help nurse her mother who had broken her hip, came back. Bobby started falling asleep at meals and looking at things with his head down but looking up, then shutting one eye and then the other. No one could imagine what was the matter with him, until fortunately our family doctor, Harold Evans, diagnosed the symptoms as sleepy sickness of which there were some other cases in the town. In most cases the patients were kept awake all the time, but Dr Evans thought it was better that he should be woken for his meals and then allowed to sleep, so we all took it in turns to keep him sufficiently awake to eat.

As it happened, Dr Evans was proved right. The other cases died or were left with brain damage. Bobby's eyes were affected, the only ill effect he suffered from that illness. He was away from school for a year, but succeeded in getting into Cambridge without difficulty. The eye problem did not arise until he was older and he now has the use of only one eye. The boys he taught – he became a schoolmaster – played him up by pretending he was not looking at them when he asked a question, the bad eye looked in the opposite direction from the good eye. "Do you mean me Sir, or Smith or Jones?" (as the case might be) but he took it all in good part. My father would never allow any of us to mention the fact that he had had sleepy sickness.

Our home at Lowestoft meant a great deal to us, especially to Ben and me as the two youngest. During the week the house really belonged to the practice, and we had to keep out of the way, downstairs anyway, but from Saturday midday the house was ours. My father played golf on Saturday afternoons, and then went for a walk to the town to buy sweets for us

45

all. My mother had to have a special kind of chocolates, woe betide if he bought the wrong ones. For us he bought a quarter pound of sweets, which were to last the week.

Sundays were a ritual. It was the only day that we could have kippers for breakfast, because of the smell. At breakfast we had to decide who would go out in the car with my father and who would go to church with Mum, of course we all wanted to go out in the car except Barbara, when she was older and had a crush on the parson. She even used to get up and go to early service. Probably Ben would have liked to go if it had been to St Margaret's church instead of St John's, which was a very dull low church service, and the architecture dismal. (St John's has been pulled down now). My mother liked the low church service, and she could walk there, St Margaret's was the other end of the town. Going in the car was fun, my father visited patients on Sunday mornings, but always ended up at Sotterly which was a farm and public house combined. The landlord De-car Blowers was a friend of his. There we could play on the farm with the Blowers children and then have ginger beer out of stone jars.

When we went to church, we were entertained by the people who sat in front of us, also the other occupier of our pew. We always tried to get there first, the hassock we had to sit on did not stretch all the way, so the first there pulled it towards their end. In front of us sat a mother and two sons, one of whom had a nervous tick and wagged his head towards one side, the other rubbed his hands together all the time. Once my mother looked along the row towards Ben, who was about seven, he was wagging his head and rubbing his hands together at the same time. After that she changed our pew further back, we were all thankful for that, we hated sitting in the front. Robert was very fond of kippers, rubbed his hands on his handkerchief after breakfast and called it kipper scent.

Sunday lunch was a feast, usually with sirloin of beef, and undercut. My father was a wonderful carver, and taught Ben, who continued the Sunday lunch tradition in his various homes afterwards.

After lunch my father retired for his weekly hot bath and body culture, during the week he had cold baths every day. Poor Alice, the cook, had to stoke up the kitchen range to get the water hot enough, quite a problem after cooking the dinner. We all collapsed by the fire eating sweets, usually fudge, which was a favourite of Ben's and the dog. Both of them looked up hopefully at the rustle of a paper bag. Then my mother and Ben played duets, even from the age of seven he was an excellent pianist. It was mostly Wagner, *Die Meistersinger,* sometimes Beethoven. At that time we had statues of Wagner, Beethoven, Brahms, all over the house. He came to Mozart and Bach at a later date.

Then a huge tea with sandwiches and cake, and either the curate from the church or one of the assistant masters from South Lodge School, or both. After that a long walk; whichever of us was at home went with my father, over the bridge and to the fish-markets which were mostly deserted on Sundays, except for the Scottish boats; they never fished on Sundays. In those days anyone could walk there, although we were the only people who did. The locals all despised the fishing, they thought it smelly, then home via the Royal Yacht Club, where the young ones had to sit in an upstairs ladies room and wait until the men finished all their drinking rounds. Then a race home where Mum would be waiting impatiently. So a cold supper and to bed in our very cold bedrooms if it was winter. We were brought up hardy.

6

Growing Up

When Ben was eight years old, he left the Miss Astles' School and went to South Lodge Preparatory School, just down the hill from our house. It took boys from seven to fourteen years old and prepared them for public school, to which they went at thirteen and fourteen. Most of the boys were boarders, but there were a few day boys from local families. Ben was one of these. He told me later that he would much rather have been a boarder, because in fact he really only slept and had breakfast at home, so it meant constant re-adjustment to home life, then school. On Sundays he had to go to church with the school.

T. J. Sewell was the headmaster when Ben was there. He was a fanatical mathematician and thought he saw a future mathematician in his new pupil, but this was not to be. Ben continued to learn the piano with Ethel Astle, although my mother was realizing that he needed more than she could give him and would soon have to have lessons in composition. Already at this early age he was composing all the time. When he was five he handed his mother a piece he had just written and asked her to play it. The story is that her look of horror after looking at it put him off temporarily. He soon recovered, however, and continued to write and by the age of eight his pieces were playable.

My mother had a friend, Audrey Alston, who was the wife of a Norfolk parson. She was a very good musician and involved with the musical life in Norwich, where my mother met her. Audrey also had a son John, the same age as Ben, who was a gifted pianist and at eight years old was playing the organ in his father's church, and this was a bond between the mothers. Audrey came to Lowestoft with John, and the two little boys played duets together, each mother thinking her son the better. Ben wanted to learn a string instrument and as Audrey was a professional viola player she started to teach him. John Alston later became Director of Music at Lancing College, Sussex.

In the autumn of 1924, when Ben was ten years old, the composer Frank Bridge, a friend of Audrey's, was coming to Norwich. A new work of Bridge's, *The Sea*, was to receive its first performance during the Norwich Festival in St Andrew's Hall. He was to stay with the Alstons. So Audrey and my mother thought they would introduce Ben to Frank and ask his advice about the boy's future. At first Frank did not want to see Ben, complaining that he was always being asked to interview young people who were supposed to show musical promise, which they rarely had. However, Audrey was insistent, and as her guest, he could hardly refuse. He had not talked to Ben for more than a few minutes when he realized that here was something quite remarkable, and agreed at once to teach him composition, and arranged with Harold Samuel, the pianist, to teach Ben piano. At that time Harold had a boy called Howard Ferguson living with him as a pupil, and wanted Ben to go and live there with them, but my parents wished him to continue his schooling and thought him too young, as Howard was a lot older. It was clear that he had been well taught by Ethel Astle.

How difficult it must have been for them to know the best course to take for their young genius. Could he make a living at music? They were inexperienced in these matters. Finally, they decided that the best thing was for Ben to continue at school like a normal boy and pass exams, in case he should ever need another profession, and go on playing games, at which he was very good. He should also stay at Lowestoft which was a healthy place, for if they allowed him to go to London, they could not watch over his health which was never very good.

As events turned out, they were right, as Ben's future achievements proved. He had a first class maths training, which probably helped his composition, and he enjoyed a carefree, happy life. One of his joys was to spend hours on the beach where we had a hut. By the hut was a concrete wall, at the base of the Cliff, part of the sea defences, and here he spent hours hitting a tennis ball against the wall. Our back garden was not large enough to have a court but later on a hard tennis court was made on the field in front of our house, someone lent us a garden nearby which was large enough to have a badminton court – battledore and shuttlecock it was called then – so there was plenty of opportunity for Ben to pursue his love of sport.

It was strange that Benjamin was such a good athlete, as well as having so many other gifts. Bobby and I were average at games; Barbara was not interested in ball games but she was a first class swimmer. At one time my father hired a rowing boat which took Barbara and Bobby out to the mile buoy, to see whether they could swim a mile back to the beach. Barbara made it, in fact swam more than a mile, as the tide took her a quarter of a mile up the coast. Bobby had to come out after a short while as he was getting very cold. Fortunately, Ben and I were not put to the "Swim-a-mile" test. We were both very thin and could not have stood the cold water long enough, but we were all good swimmers from an early age.

Neither of our parents had learnt to swim. They both spent their childhood some way from the sea and there were no swimming pools in their day. My mother nevertheless was determined to try, so that she could come in the water with all of us. My father did not attempt it. I expect he thought it would be beneath his dignity to be learning with us, but he took great interest in all our exploits and was very proud of us. Poor Mum did manage to swim enough to go from breakwater to breakwater, but one of us had to be on hand to help her stand up. She could only stand by putting her hands on the bottom first, but she really enjoyed her swimming.

We had a crazy dog called Caesar, spaniel mixture. He had a passion for water and always came in with us if it were not rough; he could not manage the waves, so he sat on the edge and howled till we were all out. When he was in with us, he swam from one to the other, making sure that we were all right, until we came out; not until the last member of the family was safely on the shore did he come out. A crowd usually collected on the cliff top to watch this performance. Caesar's passion for water could be disastrous; when we were out for a walk he would make a beeline for any water, the dirtier the better, then come lovingly back to us and shake this muck all over us.

Our beach hut was a great joy to all of us, one of a row of permanently built huts at our end of the town, for residents only. Whenever we were able, we spent all day there. Mum would bring our meals and have them with us. She made the hut very pretty with curtains, nice china, tables and chairs, etc. There was a spirit stove for heating food and water. We very often had friends staying, and there were all our local friends. Ben always had many friends of all ages and sexes. We became expert at swimming in rough seas, jumping over or going through the waves. When the tide was high below the hut, the waves broke onto the sea wall, creating a backwash. To get into the water you had to go down some steep wooden steps. It was very difficult to get in and out through the waves breaking against the wall, but we were young and daring.

Although it sounds as though there was a certain amount of music in Ben's life, with visits to Frank in London, concerts in Norwich and Lowestoft, and musical evenings at home, he told me in later life that he had longed to hear even more music. He would go to the local music shop at the north end of the town, Morlings', where he spent hours listening to records. He said they were so nice about it, though he never bought any records from them. We had no gramophone at home, because my father, again thinking to do the right thing, did not want to have "mechanical music", as he called it, in the house. He was afraid that if it came too easily to us, we (or rather my brothers) would stop making our own music.

Later I bought a portable gramophone, so that I could hear my favourite light music. I did not care for classical music in those days, although I do now. Our father finally relented and in 1930 he bought a radiogram, a large cabinet with gramophone at the top and radio underneath. This was really too late for Ben to hear all the music he needed at an early age, for by that time he was at the Royal College of Music in London. Wireless, as radio was called then, was in its very early stages when we were growing up. Some of our friends had crystal sets which they made themselves. None of us was mechanically minded enough to want to do that and in any case, the sound was not good enough to hear music properly.

When we were young we had very little pocket money, a penny a week as I remember. We were encouraged to save this and put it each week in our money boxes, so that when Christmas and birthdays came round, we had money with which to buy presents. When the time came to buy presents for people, my money box was nearly empty. Ben was always good with money and somehow always managed to have some. He was never mean, and was the first to give anything away, but rarely spent anything on himself. Bobby and I were always the spendthrifts in the family, and this continued into later life. Barbara and Ben always seemed to have money, Bobby and I never.

My father was not a mean man, but expenses weighed heavily on him. He had four children to educate and there were no grants in those days. He knew also that we should all have to go away to boarding schools. The Lowestoft schools were adequate only up to the age of thirteen but government schools in small towns in those days did not offer much in the way of further education. In any case by standards then it would have been unthinkable in our parents' eyes for us to go to them; apart from lack of tuition, an element of pure snobbery also forbade it. Certainly expenses must have been very heavy while we were all being educated; Ben at preparatory school, Bobby at public school, then on to Cambridge, Barbara training in London, and I at my girls' public school.

My mother liked the good things of life, a comfortable home and nice clothes and had a passion for antiques, for which we all had cause to be grateful later. When one of us was taking her out in the car (that is, when we were old enough to drive), Pop would whisper to us as we left the house "Keep her away from the antique shops". There was a favourite one in Southwold that she liked to go to. But I am sure we could not "keep her away". She was a very determined lady. My father appreciated the comfortable home that she made and the fact that she was always well dressed, but like so many men he thought a lot of things unnecessary. One of his wise sayings was: "Don't think what you want, think what you can do without". He certainly managed without new clothes. His tailor was Masterson, who had a shop in London Road South and the suits cost £6 each. He made them last for years. Ben wore his father's tails and his morning suit until he was over forty and always looked extremely good in them. My son borrowed the morning suit for weddings several times.

One day when Ben was four or five my mother had to go to the tailor on some errand, she had Ben with her, she was talking to the tailor and suddenly realized everything was very quiet; there was another woman in the shop with a small girl. My mother turned round to look and, to her horror, Ben had got the tailor's huge scissors and the little girl was cowering in the corner with Ben advancing towards her with the scissors open.

My father used to say things to us such as "Make money, honestly if you can", or "Don't marry money but go where money is". My mother would be horrified and say "Robert, don't say things like that to the children, you know you don't mean it". He certainly was the most honest man, but overcome with the need to make ends meet.

In spite of our father's anxiety about finance, there was never any question of exploiting Ben. My parents did not want him to perform in public. But what a draw he could have been: at the age of eight he was already a brilliant pianist and looked so charming with his golden curls and blue eyes. He could also have played his own compositions. They determined that at whatever cost Ben should be allowed to grow up naturally and that no pressure should be put on him. It is certain that people would not have liked Ben's compositions then. He was considered very *avant garde* in those early days. My mother once said to a friend of hers: "I do wish Benjamin would write something that people like." He was about fifteen at the time. In fact, he wrote several very tuneful pieces, such as *Beware* and later used tunes composed at nine and ten, in the *Simple Symphony*. The *Beware* manuscript he gave to me and I proudly took it to my boarding school and showed it to my music teacher, Miss Ward, saying my little brother had composed it. She could not have been less interested, and barely glanced at it. I have wondered later if she regretted the incident when he had become famous.

I was amazed when I first arrived at the school, St. Anne's, Abbots Bromley, following after my sister Barbara, that I was asked how Barbara was getting on with her music; they considered her very promising. I thought their standard must be very low, for she was not thought good at home, but they had no idea what else we had in the music line at our house. My father wanted me to give up learning the piano, as it was a waste of time and money, but my mother stuck to her guns. She said I should have the same chance as the others. I did not benefit, I fear.

At South Lodge School the hours were very long; the headmaster was a fanatic and worked the little boys very hard. In Ben's case he had to contend with his mother. If she thought her ewe lamb was being ill-treated or overworked down the hill she would run in order to protest. She insisted always that he must have time to practise and write his music. This was very frustrating for the teacher, who wanted great academic results and scholarships for the honour of his school. It must have been especially maddening when Ben after the age of eleven was taken from school during term time to go to London for lessons with Frank Bridge and Harold Samuel.

The lessons with Frank were a great strain on Ben. Frank in his enthusiasm would forget that he was teaching a child and would have kept on for hours had not my mother, anxiously waiting outside the room, interrupted the lesson. She told us that Ben would come out blinking and twitching nervously, and white with exhaustion. When he was under strain Ben had a habit of blinking his eyes with a sort of nervous tic, but of course he loved learning from Frank and benefited greatly from these lessons.

Frank was a great enthusiast and a tremendous talker and Ben was so advanced and knowledgeable musically that Frank forgot he was a young boy. The London visits occurred two or three times a term and usually once during the holidays. While Mum and Ben were in London they always went to a concert or two. Barbara was working in London then, and they stayed either with her or with friends.

It was as if from that time Ben had two fathers; his own father, "Pop", at home, and Frank Bridge in London, his musical father, who guided him in his compositions and in music generally. Ben's real father and his musical father were poles apart. Frank was the popular idea of an artist in those days. He had long hair, was very excitable and talked a lot. Our father was very conservative and could not stand anyone who talked as much, thinking it showed an empty mind. Fortunately they did not often meet, except on the rare occasions when our father went to London. The Bridges never came to Lowestoft. However, they must have met in Norwich, when Frank's new piece, *Enter Spring*, was performed at the 1927 Norwich Festival, on October 27th. I cannot imagine my father enjoyed it, and there was practically a riot in St Andrew's Hall on that occasion. The piece was considered so modern few could tolerate it. My father left everything concerned with Ben's musical education to Mum and attended only to the rest of his education.

Ben certainly excelled himself in his last years at prep. school. He became Captain of the school, Captain of cricket, and Victor Ludorum in the school sports. To see him running was the funniest thing. His feet were large and very flat; he did not appear to be going fast, but he certainly got there.

Front row, left to right. Grandma Charlotte Britten-Ginders (mother), Julianne Britten, Effie Hockey (sisters), Edith (the bride), Robert (the bridegroom), Queenie Hockey (sister), Aunt Julia Ginders.

Back row, left to right. Frederick Hockey (brother), Nellie Britten (sister), Grandpa the Rev. William Hockey (father), (an uncle), Florence and Jessie Britten (sisters), Daisy Hockey (sister) Edward Britten (brother), Janie and Willie Hockey (sister-in-law and brother).

Robert Victor Britten, Benjamin's father. 1909.

Edith Rhoda Britten, Benjamin's mother. 1909.

Grandma Rhoda Hockey with granddaughter Barbara. 1903.

Grandma Charlotte Britten with granddaughter Beth. 1909.

Edward (left) and Robert (right) Britten, uncle and father of Benjamin.

Ben, Kit Welford and Lennox Berkeley. Peasenhall Hall, July 1937.

Parents' engagement picture, 1900.

Holiday boy, July 1938. (Photo: Kit Welford.)

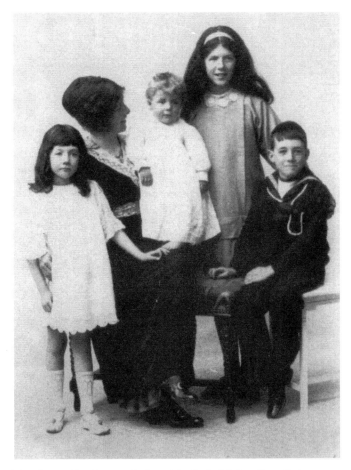

Top: Britten Family, 1914. Left to right: Beth, Mother, Ben, Barbara and Bobby.

At Sebastian's wedding, July 1966. Left to right: Barbara, Robert, Beth and Ben.

Ben, Mother and Beth, 1917.

Cinderella at Lowestoft, 1916. Top row left Barbara, third left Robert, bottom row left Beth, second left Ben.

"The Flying Scotsman" drawing by Ben aged six.

Ben aged about ten.

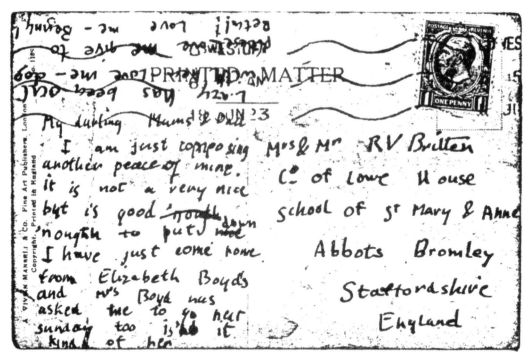

PRINTED MATTER

POSTAGE REVENUE
ONE PENNY

My darling Mums & Dad

I am just composing
another peace of mine.
it is not a very nice
but is good 'nough
'nough to put down
I have just come home
from Elizabeth Boyds
and mrs Boyd was
asked me to go her
sunday too is it
kind of her

Mrs & Mr RV Britten
C. of Lowe House
School of St Mary & Anne
Abbots Bromley
Staffordshire
England

A postcard from Ben to his parents who were visiting Beth at boarding school, dated June 18th, 1923.

Aldeburgh Music Club rehearsal at Crag House, Ben's home. Left to right: Imogen Holst (Ben's music assistant), Benjamin, and Mary Potter (artist, who exchanged houses with Ben and Peter: Crag House/Red House. See page 192).

7

Public School

When Ben was thirteen and it was time for him to leave South Lodge, the question was "What next?" He wanted to go to London and get on with music. There was a family meeting. His parents were half in mind to let him have his way but his elder brother and sister thought not. They said Ben must have more schooling, for, as they said: "How could anyone be sure that he could make a living at music alone?" He should go to a public school long enough to pass the School Certificate. I can remember clearly the heated discussion that took place in the drawing room, Barbara and Bobby arguing that in any case he was too young to be let loose in London. They had their way. It was decided that he should go on to public school until he had taken School Certificate, as soon as possible, and then the situation should be reviewed.

The school chosen was Gresham's School, Holt, in those days considered to be an advanced school, although not particularly musical. That did not matter, as Ben would be continuing his lessons for piano and composition in London. He won a musical scholarship for his education at Gresham's of £30 a year, which delighted us although it was not much. The music master was not pleased when he was told that Ben would not be learning music at school. When the music master first met Ben, he said "So you are the boy who likes Stravinsky!" Years later Ben was talking to a boy from that school who had been in trouble because he had liked Britten's music.

In September 1928 when Ben was due to go to Gresham's, I was in France learning the language, and very homesick. My father wrote constantly telling me all the news at home.

On September 13th he wrote (he was in bed):

> . . . Beni has just been in to say goodnight, he says he will write to you on Sunday. He has a wonderful new trunk, hold the house I think. We hope to go to Holt on Tuesday afternoon to see Mr. Eccles [the headmaster] and then take Beni on Thursday.

On September 22nd he writes again:

> We took the "Captain" on Thursday (we shall know that road soon, twice last week we went) and his letter seems to show he is not too homesick; he is in the choir – with that voice! [His voice was breaking].

Ben did not tell his parents what happened to him at Gresham's at the beginning of his first term. His mother at any rate would have had a fit if she had known. In those days, at public schools, new boys had horrid things done to them. From what Ben told me later, he was thrown in a blanket and then into water. Luckily for him he fainted, so the senior boys who were the tormentors stopped in fright and thereafter he was left in peace.

On October 21st, Pop writes to me, in France:

> Barbara is here. We had fixed to go to Beni yesterday and on Tuesday Barbara wrote to say she was coming home for the weekend (we hadn't asked her!). So we arranged for her to go to Norwich and we to meet her and so go on to Holt. Everything panned out as arranged – we met her and arrived at Gresham's school, one o'c. Sat: met your brother the Captain, went out, had lunch on the road, went on to Sheringham, a very pretty little place, and on to nearby Cromer, came back, had tea, back to Holt; Beni showed Barbara over the school, left him at 5.30. Good drive back to Lowestoft, and found our lovely drawing room with a glorious fire all by itself. Beni seems wonderfully happy and to have settled down well. His study is quite grand, very different from Robert's at Oakham.
> He has come out top of his form at the monthly exams they have – we are very bucked of course – as he went there with rather a weight of learning to live up to."

Ben's house at Gresham's, Farfield House, had a temporary housemaster in his first two terms. He was a bachelor and the boys fed like fighting cocks. The feeding system at most public schools then was that the housemasters were given a lump sum with which they fed their boys. The result was if the master's wife was at all unscrupulous she did not spend all the given money on the boys but kept some for themselves and as a result the boys were starved or had to provide their own food. My husband was at Charterhouse and he told me that all they had to eat after lunch was a single bun. They had to find their own suppers, either from the tuck shop or from food they brought back to school with them. Fortunately this system was changed later and when my son went to Lancing College, a Woodard school, the boys were fed from a central kitchen.

My mother continued to go to London with Ben when he first went to Gresham's, at any rate for the first term, until she dared let him go alone and felt she could trust Frank not to exhaust Ben.

My father wrote to me on November 11th 1928:

> Mum has been up in Town with Beni; he went up for a lesson with Frank Bridge and Harold Samuel. They met at Ipswich but had to come back separate ways; they had a very good time and most successful. All three, Mum, Barbara and Beni, went to a concert at Queen's Hall.
>
> I went with Mum down to the two minutes' silence this morning at the Royal Plain, we went to the top of the Club [Yacht] to see it – it was a very well done affair I thought, Mum ought to have been with the Musical Society but when we got there it was impossible to find them or go through the crowd. I wonder if they have anything like it in France?
>
> I ought not to be writing to you really – Robert says he never gets a letter from me – Beni the same – and Barbara says "It's nothing but your wonderful daughter Beth." But then you are out in heathen countries full of savages and wild beasts, but it won't be long now and then I'll tuck you up …
>
> They (our people) are all upstairs – Bobby playing, can you guess, well no – I'll tell you! – Ragtimes!
>
> Cheerio! my daughter, keep the English character up.

My father continued to call Ben Beni for a while. I suppose he found it hard to realize that he was fifteen and already very mature.

When I returned home from France in November 1928, Ben was of course still at Gresham's. He enjoyed the summers there when he could play cricket and tennis but he was not allowed to play football or hockey on account of his heart condition, so during the winter afternoons he could amuse himself as he chose. There was a good music room at the school where he could play records or practise the piano. He was also composing all the time by now.

I stayed at home for two years. My father said he ought to be allowed to have one child at home, out of four, and as I was not academic it seemed to have to be me. Although my father loved to have me at home, it was an aimless existence. I had to do boring chores, such as dust the drawing room before breakfast, chilly to say the least in the winter, the fire was not lit until lunch time. My father had misguidedly imagined that I should take over the running of the house and do the cooking, he was very anxious that I should learn to cook. In the meantime my mother and Alice, the cook, should sit back and have a rest. This did not please either of them.

It was good for me when Ben was home for the holidays. We could do things together, go to tennis and beach parties, he was always so much easier than I was with people, and had lots of friends of both sexes. My mother was a bit of a snob and there were people in "trade" she did not like us to know; however Ben overruled all that and mixed with anyone he liked. When he was at prep school there were two little girls who loved him dearly. One was a very pretty good little girl, Winnie Rix (see family photo in the garden at Lowestoft) and the other a very pretty not so good little girl, with a sophisticated mother, who had little control over her children. Once when one of her children had been naughty she appealed to my mother who told her to keep the child in for punishment. "Oh, I can't do that, I am going out to play bridge". Ben wavered between the two of them, they exchanged wedding rings. One day when the not so good one had displeased him, he told my mother that she was like a rosy apple with a rotten inside.

My father's dental practice spread for miles around Lowestoft, and he liked us to socialise with the patients. So as soon as I could drive which I did when I was seventeen, I drove my mother and Ben, when he was at home to all the social gatherings. My father always had the fear that he was losing patients. He was as busy as usual, too hard-working, but he had the dread that he could not meet the family bills. Robert was at this time at Cambridge and being very extravagant and not working too much. We dreaded the rows when he came home. Barbara was working then in London, so she was more or less off his hands.

8

First Years in London

When Ben was sixteen he passed School Certificate and, at the end of the summer term in July 1930, he left Gresham's. Earlier in the summer he went to London to sit for a written paper examination for an Open Scholarship in the concert hall of the Royal College of Music. Bernard Richards, the cellist, who was also taking this examination, told me that, while waiting to go in, he chatted to a likeable young man who said his name was Benjamin Britten. They were allotted three hours for the paper which was on the rudiments of music and a bit of harmony. After twenty minutes this same Benjamin Britten took his paper up to the invigilator, who could not believe that it was finished. Bernard said there was quite a little scene and the invigilator insisted that Ben went back and checked the answers. This he did for another five minutes or so and then left. After Bernard told me this story I asked Ben if he remembered this occasion. He said he did and added that they were not very nice about it. He won a scholarship to the College, so he must have got it right!

Having been accepted as a student at the Royal College, the next thing was to find somewhere for Ben to live in London. He went first to a boarding house in Bayswater, so that he would only have to cross Kensington Gardens to get to the College. It was not too far from Frank and Ethel Bridge, who had a house just off Church Street, Kensington.

The scholarship he won was for free tuition, but money for board and lodging had to be found. John Ireland was allotted as his composition teacher and Arthur Benjamin his piano teacher. Neither Frank nor Harold Samuel were on the staff of the College.

Ben did not enjoy learning from John Ireland, who was not sympathetic to the young composer. Sometimes Ben had to go to Ireland's flat for his lessons and very often he was still in bed, often with a hangover, and the place was in a mess, with dirty milk bottles piled up outside. That disgusted Ben, who was always extremely neat and tidy in his person and in the places where he lived. He was never the popular idea of a musician or artist at that time, with long untidy hair and messy clothes.

He was not happy at the College, most of the time he was bored and frustrated, by having to do elementary exercises, while he was bursting with ideas and compositions. Opportunities of having these works performed at the College were non-existent. Only one of Ben's works was played at the College during the whole three years he was there, and that was his *Sinfonietta (Op.1)* for ten instruments, which was included in the programme of a chamber music concert on 16th March 1933, more than two months after it had received its first performance elsewhere.

Ben was happy learning the piano from Arthur Benjamin, whom he liked very much. Arthur was sympathetic to him. He passed the examination for the Associateship of the College as a solo pianist in 1933 with flying colours. Having won the Ernest Farrar Prize for composition, he was also given a small travelling scholarship when he left the College in July 1933, and wanted to go to Vienna to study with Alban Berg. He always felt bitter that his parents, or most probably his mother, did not want him to go. He thought Sir Hugh Allen, who was then Director at the College, put a spoke in the wheel and persuaded his mother that Berg would not be a good influence for Ben at that time, and she had probably heard about Berg's private life. His parents always tried so hard to do the right thing for him and mostly they succeeded but this time he felt they had failed him.

The Bridges had a house in Friston near Eastbourne as well as their London house, where they went most weekends, often taking Ben with them while he was in London. It was a charming house with a tennis court, on top of the downs. A dear friend of theirs, Margery Fass, had a house next door; she also was a very good musician, so they were in and out of each other's houses most of the time. In the summer it was great fun, with swimming expeditions, tennis, and picnics in different parts of Sussex. Although Ben loved these weekends and enjoyed the countryside, nothing to him was as beautiful and satisfying as his beloved Suffolk, with the wilder scenery and the estuaries with their variety of birds and waders.

What Ben loved most at Friston was the music and companionship. Each evening, and when the weather was not fine enough to go out, Ethel and Frank and any friends they had staying would play together. Frank was a professional viola player and Ethel a violinist. Ben was playing the viola well by that time, so when he was not at the piano, he played the viola. Many musicians came to stay. Two young friends of Ben's at the College, Bernard Richards, cellist, and Remo Lauricella, violinist, were often invited to stay the weekend and join in the music-making. Later when I was in London I used to go as well. I could not join in the music making but would sit and knit and listen. It was a joke with the players: if I stopped knitting, they would say: "We must be good, Beth has stopped knitting".

Ethel and Frank were warm and hospitable and dear and funny. It was a tragedy that they had no children. She was also a marvellous housewife. Both the London house and the Sussex house were charming and however many people turned up for meals or to stay, there was never any fuss. She was particularly kind to us young ones and of course especially to Ben, for they loved him as a son. What joy he must have brought to them in their later years. Ethel was an Australian, who had come to England to study the violin, and met Frank and married him. It was always said that they were the happiest married couple in the musical world. The fact that Marg Fass who lived next door seemed to be a part of the menage and adored Frank did not seem to worry her.

Ethel and I used to discuss the fact that we were the healthiest people in our families. She told me that she used to long to be ill, as I indeed did, and that when she was in her teens she lay on wet grass all night, hoping that some illness would befall her so she would get sympathy from her family. Nothing happened, she remained as healthy as ever.

Frank had very bushy hair which he let grow long, it stuck out all over his head. The first time I went swimming with them, I was amazed to see an extraordinary person with us looking just like a walrus. It was Frank who had dived under the water and come up with his hair streaming down his face.

The Bridges had a car; Ben swore that they were the worst drivers he had ever driven with. Frank was even more excitable when he was in charge of a car than usual, seeming to think that everyone was against him. I remember driving back with them to Kensington Church Street after a concert one fairly foggy night. Frank and Ethel were in front, Ben and I behind. They were leaning out of their windows calling to each other about how near the curb was and going oh, so slowly, until all the other cars were flashing past us. We were so ashamed.

It was a sadness to Ben that Frank did not have the recognition as a composer and conductor that Ben felt he should have had. Perhaps Frank had not the push required. Ben considered him to be a fine conductor.

The other day I went to see Miss Elsie Bernard, who told me how she used to play the violin in Audrey Chapman's Orchestra in London. She said that Frank Bridge was their usual conductor and told me how they all loved him. He demanded a lot from them and in his enthusiasm he inspired fine playing from them all. Elsie related how on one occasion he was conducting with such energy and became so hot that some of his collar studs flew off on to her lap.

As I was getting restless at home, and hating the social round, I wanted to be up and doing and have a career as Barbara had done. The only thing I was any good at was making clothes. My father relented, but what to do? He had a friend who was the owner of the Wentworth Hotel in Aldeburgh, Suffolk, who also had a daughter about to take up dress design. My father said he would go and talk to him.

Our parents were very fond of Aldeburgh and often stayed at the Wentworth Hotel there. Our father was a keen golfer and loved the Aldeburgh course. He little thought when he was playing on that course that one day his younger son Benjamin would make his home at the Red House, whose garden is only separated from the Aldeburgh course by a lane. Ben's father must have passed the Red House dozens of times.

I went to the Paris Academy of Dressmaking and Design in Bond Street so that I was in London while Ben was still at the College.

Ben was not happy at his lodgings in Bayswater, so it was finally decided that we should go together to a boarding house in London, Burleigh House, 173 Cromwell Road. This was a very tall Victorian house and we had two rooms at the very top. When our father took us there, the first thing he did was to find the fire escape, which was cluttered up with boxes and trunks. He insisted that it should be cleared and saw to it that this was done before he left.

Ben's room was a little larger than mine because he had to have a piano. Even so, it was crowded. There was the baby grand, a table large enough for him to compose on, a chair, a bedside table and a bed. When it got very hot in the summer, as it did on the top floor, he would take a blanket or two and sleep on the piano. Ben was still at the College then and, although he went there most days, he was working a lot on his own. After the fire escape was cleared we could get out on to the roof where we often sat on summer days, although it was very dirty up there.

Bernard Richards and Lauricella often came and played trios with Ben in his room, tiny though it was. Bernard told me how Ben and he and his sister, who was a violinist, went down to Lowestoft once to give a concert in St. John's Church. On the way down by train they were rather bored, so Ben amused them by writing a round for them to sing, on paper he had got from the gents' toilet. He wrote it so that the two sitting opposite could read it from their side without turning the paper. Bernard said he wished he had kept the flimsy paper, but it was thrown away. The concert in the church was a great success. Ben and I stayed on together in Cromwell Road for eighteen months, setting out together in the mornings for our respective training establishments, he to the Royal College, I to the Paris Academy. We had quite a lot of fun on the top floor of the boarding house, there were five rooms up there and it was either young people like ourselves or older people who could afford only the cheaper rooms. The lift only went three floors up, to the more expensive rooms, so we had to slog the rest of the way.

On May 26th 1932 our father wrote to Ben and me at Burleigh House, Cromwell Road. He was in bed in the spare room at home, in fact the start of his final, fatal illness:.

Spareroom.

My two dear brave children, both so great and yet so different – my love to thee both.

This is to be a labour-saving letter. I really haven't time to write to you separately as you will well understand, besides I always believe in labour saving. Mum is having a hectic day: she popped home about six o'clock for half an hour to tell me how things were going; apparently wonderfully well, crowds of people congratulated her personally. It's been a fine day for them too. There was a slight uneasiness with the Jagos. You know they were doing the incidental music (whatever that is). Well! Mrs. Jago didn't like Mr. Colman accompanying Mum in their bit and said "Oh! I suppose I'm not good enough", etc, etc. Having heard her in "The Ship" – do you remember? – I rather think you will agree with me saying quite right, quite right.

It's a good thing I am writing as I've quite forgotten how to talk – I've got good books though. There is no news I can tell you. You know the room I am in and what it's like so its no good describing it. It's just the same except for a lovely bowl of Lillies, or Lillys. If they were only a little farther off I would draw them and send you the picture, then you could have it framed with some of your excessive pocket money – I've been thinking what can they do with it all? – I believe you Ben must be running a theatre or something with all yours. By–the–way, I saw a funny bit the other day about Gerald du Maurier (talking of theatres made me think of it) that he chooses his friends by their ties or their titles – he is supposed to be a bit of a snob isn't he?

Now you are dying to hear about me. Well! I think I may be a bit better, I don't know. The pain has certainly been better today but the temp keeps bobbing about like Caesar [our Clumber spaniel] in that pond near the Kessingland Road. The doctor hasn't been for two days. He came this afternoon, but no fear! the King had left word that he was not to be disturbed until he rang and he wasn't (talk of Russia in the old days).

Ruby has just been in hissing like escaping steam to draw the blinds so I can no longer see the Boyds' back door, the only thing that raised me out of the encircling gloom is gone, oh dear! oh dear!

How is Miss Wrist? (I haven't had the receipt yet) and all the others? And ah! important words! how is *the work?* I expect you feel very strange Beth going back to Bond St. It comes very hard getting into fixed hours again.

We are going in for the D. Mail £3,000 Derby Sweep and I've been working them out. I've filled up nine forms, four places for four horses & 23 horses – it's not half as easy as it sounds – I've studied the history of each horse, I've got two more to do, Friday and Saturday.

I'm glad the concert went well on Sunday and that my two were heard above and in front of all the others. I hear you have another this Sunday.

Goodnight my two. It's getting late and a bit eerie. I swear that the wardrobe door is beginning to open slowly and there seems to be a sort of sighing coming from it. Is it only mice, I wonder, or something more terrible? What ought I to do I wonder.

So long! two of my treasures, a grand and useful life to both of you with health and happiness.

Your very loving father "Pop"

R. V. Britten

We had made friends with an old lady called Miss Wrist, who had a top floor room. She probably was not very old but she seemed so to us. She wore very thick glasses which magnified her eyes and made her look very old, but she was great fun and came to stay with us in Lowestoft several times.

Ben's vacations were long and he went home to Lowestoft as often as he could, finding it much easier to write by his beloved sea. The old nursery had been turned into his study-bedroom and since Bobby was married he had the room to himself. There was a table by the window so Ben had an uninterrupted view of the sea and the harbour, and could watch the boats going to and fro.

When Ben was in London on Sundays we usually took a bus to St. Stephen's Walbrook, the Wren church in the City, where the Rector, the Rev. Mr. Clark, was a friend of ours. After the service we would walk back through the City, then along the Embankment to Westminster and on through St. James's Park to Hyde Park, Kensington Gardens, past the Albert Hall and so home. We both had an appetite for Sunday lunch by that time. In the afternoons, if it was fine, we walked again to Kensington Gardens and watched the model yachts on the Round Pond.

Sometimes in the evenings we went separate ways, but often we went together to a film or the opera. Ben was mad about the Marx brothers, Charles Chaplin and the Disney films. There was a cinema in St Martin's Lane where Disney films were running continuously, so we often went there – it was cheap and neither of us had much pocket money.

Ben, who had a love for Wagner at the time, said he wanted to take me to Wagner's Opera *Tristan and Isolde*, so when it was next on at Covent Garden, we went. As usual, we queued for the gallery, the only place we could afford – it cost one shilling and sixpence. He warned me that the famous love duet between Tristan and Isolde was so emotional that people had been known to be physically sick when hearing it, so I must not be surprised if I felt ill. Actually I did not feel ill, which I think disappointed him rather. It was so uncomfortable in the gallery: one sat on benches so narrow and so close together that the knees of the people sitting behind stuck into one's back; also the stage seemed so far away that it was difficult to see and hear very clearly.

We got to know almost all the galleries in London's theatreland. The method was to go early and book a stool for sixpence – there was an old man in charge. Then we went away and had a meal somewhere, coming back to retrieve our places at least half an hour before the doors opened and the stools were removed. Most of the galleries cost one shilling and threepence, but the pit cost three shillings and sixpence and we rarely could afford that. At each queue there were the buskers or street entertainers, who sang or did acrobatics and then came along with their hats. There was one man with long streaming hair, which was remarkable in the thirties, who just walked the length of each queue and then went on to the next. He did not collect any money. I saw him in the City too, I suppose he spent all day walking about rather fast.

One evening I had been up in West London with some friends and coming back I had to change buses at Hyde Park Corner. There I was accosted by a man and I could not get rid of him. I hoped he would not get on the same bus as I did, but he did and all the way I worried what to do if he got off the bus with me at my stop. To my joy, as I got off, there stood Ben. For some unknown reason he had come to meet me, which was quite extraordinary, as he could not have known when I was coming, and the man stayed on the bus when he saw I had a male protector, not a very tough one, but enough!

I told my father about this incident thinking he would be pleased. He always seemed to think that Barbara and I had not enough followers – he wanted us to get married, so that we would have someone to look after us when he had gone. Nonetheless, he was furious about my being accosted and worried about my going about alone so that I wished I had not told him. Once in a letter to me my father wrote: "I am glad you have Benjamin to look after you – he's a remarkable chap for looking after people".

Barbara had a suitor, although she did not realize that he was intending marriage. She thought he brought her presents and took her out because he was a friend of her father's. He was indeed a golfing friend of his, certainly a few years older than she was, but then her father was only twenty-three years older than Barbara. This man, Gerald, a District Commissioner in West Africa, was what could be considered a good match for any girl. In 1928 brother Bobby was up at Cambridge. Our parents planned to visit him, Gerald was to drive Barbara from London to Cambridge and they would all have a jolly weekend there. Halfway between London and Cambridge, Gerald stopped the car and proposed marriage. Barbara, completely taken aback with shock and horror, jumped out of the car and fled down the road; but she had to come back to the car as they were some way from Cambridge and it was too far to walk. They had a miserable weekend. Her father was furious with her for refusing to marry Gerald. She told him she did not love him, that in fact he sent cold shivers down her back, and anyway she did not want to live in Africa. "You need not have gone to Africa", said her father, "you could have stayed at home with us and just gone with him when he came on leave". Anyway her mother supported her, for she did not think Gerald would make Barbara happy, he was too silent and stiff. It was quite long before she was forgiven by her father for refusing such an excellent arrangement. He was not content, however, when Bobby became engaged at the age of twenty-three. He thought him foolish to take on the responsibilities of a family so young. Our father was already suffering from the illness that killed him and probably realized he had not long to live and was consequently concerned for our futures.

When I had finished my dressmaking training in London, I left the boarding house in Cromwell Road and, with a girl I had met at the Academy, Lilian Wolff, rented two floors over a grocer's at 559 Finchley Road, Hampstead. We set up in business there as Elspeth Beide, a dressmaking establishment. (The name came of our both having the name Elizabeth; *beide* is German for "both".) I had now to earn my own living. We let off the top floor and used the large front room as a workroom and the one next to it as a fitting room; the small room at the back was my bed-sitting room, with a put-you-up bed and a gas ring for cooking.

In a letter written to me on February 19th 1933 my father says:

> I do believe you will make good, Beth. A brave heart and a level head.
> Please ask me anything you want to know.
> I hope to get up soon.
> It's been a beautiful day if you didn't go out; snow and all that but a bitter wind. I took Caesar over the Links [golf] and although it was covered with snow there were two loonies playing . . . Tell Ben I heard his "little piece" and enjoyed it. I'll write to him later . . .

Our fathers contributed £100 each to start us off. After we had equipped ourselves with the necessary sewing machines, tables, mirrors, furniture for the fitting room, etc., and sent out advertising pamphlets to people in the neighbourhood, there was very little of the £200 left. We engaged two girls, an improver and an apprentice. The apprentice made the tea, swept the floors and answered the door to customers, in fact made herself useful. She was allowed to do simple tacking and so on. The improver did more difficult sewing and ironing.

Then we sat back waiting hopefully for the customers to roll in. In the meantime we had to pay the girls, pay the rent, gas and electricity, and keep ourselves. It was easier for Lilian as she was living at home and did not have to pay her parents for her keep. I started to go out for one meal a day, but soon had to stop that for it was too expensive. It was difficult to cook much on my gas ring and in any case I was no cook. Then Lilian's mother suggested that Lilian should bring each day, in a workman's pot, the remains of what the Wolffs had had the night before for dinner. That was fine for me, it was very good food; the Wolffs had a chef and he sent some tasty meals. I practically lived on that. I was determined if possible to keep myself, but actually I was laying the seeds of the later illness that nearly killed me and killed my mother.

My father was worried because he thought Lilian was too young – she was five years younger than me – and he thought that because she did not have to work she might not pull her weight in this new venture. The Wolff family were well-off and she was the only precious daughter. In fact, she worked hard and was always a great help in every way. We divided the work because we thought it better to have our own departments. Lilian readily did the fitting and the sewing and overseeing of the girls, while I did the cutting.

The money was too slow coming in so we had to appeal to our fathers for more and they each sent us fifty pounds. Our mothers helped by giving us orders – we dressed them almost entirely and they did us credit by wearing our clothes. Even with the extra money from the fathers, however, I did not have enough to live on, although I had no intention of telling my parents, I was determined to manage. Nevertheless, sister Barbara seemed to know and she told our parents. My father wrote (October 13th 1933):

> For thirty years I have kept my family, though maybe only on bread and water, so that it came as a bad shock to know that our elegant, so affable daughter was actually in want. Why on earth didn't you let us know? Mum would have gone without her "patte de fois gras" (sic) and I would have gone without my Bournevita (could I, I wonder) before you should have gone hungry. I hope you got the two pounds from Benjamin today. I will send up some more by Barbara.
>
> Barbara arrived midday, she doesn't look too bad I think. I haven't been to Southwold today and oh! I am so grateful "Mum" and I went shopping this morning, as they brought the car round in the usual Friday way . . . . .

My mother added a postscript:

Darling Child

If you are short another time, send at once, and if you don't – can't – feed and dress properly let us know. What is money for – if not to help our children? When you come home next time we'll make a proper arrangement. Pop seems much less tired today and we have quite cheered up. Tell Benj. that we are feeling a little brighter. He is very anxious I know! as of course you and we all are.

By the bye, Barbara is quite right to tell us, I should be very upset not to know.

I hope you will have a nice happy weekend and get out for some lovely walks. The Heath ought to be lovely now. My love to you darling child and take care of yourself.

Your Mum.

9

Father's Illness and Death

As can be seen from these letters our father was getting increasingly ill. No doctor could find out what was wrong with him. He saw a specialist in Ipswich. He was furious because the doctor charged him five pounds and, as he said, did nothing. He had no faith in doctors, he said he had seen too much of their ways in his work. Barbara, Ben and I kept finding new remedies which we thought would help, and were desperately anxious about him. Pop was so good and he patiently tried all these remedies. We three in London arranged things so that one of us would go home every weekend. It was a great strain on our mother, who was being so brave; and also it gave him great pleasure to have us at home. Benjamin, fortunately, was able to be in Lowestoft more than Barbara or I, as we were tied up in our jobs, while he was more often free.

On September 9th 1933 Pop wrote to me:

> We are all the same here. It's a cold wind blowing out of the North. The apes and females are all rushing to put on their clothes – no more nakedness now for a year. Mum and Ben are upstairs. Ben has some awful noisy stuff on the wireless which he calls "good" music. I managed to walk down to the Club tonight and – after countless "gins" – managed to walk back. I do so hope you will make a success of things, Beth. Your skill I don't doubt; but that isn't all that is necessary, so many other things go to the making of a successful business. Good luck to you!
>
> I am going upstairs now and will finish this tomorrow.
>
> Sunday morning. Blessed day!
>
> I am just going for a short walk with Ben and dog and then Ben is going to church with Mum. So long, my daughter! Courage, my dear.
> Your very loving father
> R. V. Britten

After the specialist decreed that Pop had an ulcer and must have only fish or white meat, we all lived on fish. Of course, we were in the right place for fish. My mother found a marvellous variety, some we had never heard of, and Alice the cook took enormous trouble to make all the fish dishes extra tasty. She loved my father, as did everyone in the house, and was concerned that he was so ill. He was always so considerate of the maids as well as the family.

Bobby was far away in Wales, where he and his wife Marjorie had bought a run-down boys' preparatory school and were having to work hard to build it up again. It was therefore difficult for him to get away, but on November 18th 1933 Pop wrote:

> ... Mum is just off to meet Ben. I hope he caught the train, 8.15 he said .... My cough is ever so much better, astonishingly so, I hardly cough or "spit" now at all.... Robert has written to say he is coming next Friday and alone – what a conquest! I don't know how long for.

> It's beastly weather, dark and wet and windy ... Goodbye my Beth.

The cough to which he refers came back again and he got weaker and weaker but still struggled to go on working. He had an enlarged heart among other things, but refused operations and hospitalisation. He was just fifty-seven when he died. On December 19th 1933, our father was still struggling to write. He says:

> My beautiful daughter Beth
>   I am awfully sorry things are so bad with you; although as you are busy it is not serious. I am enclosing a cheque for £5, partly to get some food and partly to buy yourself something for Xmas. Isn't old Ben a wonder? And so modest about it all. It's very dull and dark here now. I'm drinking your stuff but it's very uninteresting. I'm sick of it.
>   Goodbye Beth. I expect Mum will fill up the rest.

>   Your very loving Father (Pop).

Mum writes on the back of his letter:

I do hope you haven't been starving. These troublesome times will pass as soon as these wretched back bills are paid. I'd like to pay them all for you. But keep up your courage and all will be well. Benjamin said you wanted clothes for a present, perhaps you can get something out of the £5 beside paying your week's food. Pop isn't worse; we've been making him try with the herbal stuff. He has taken a few glasses which I made myself . . . . . Saturday will soon be here and you will be very welcome at home. We may not meet the train, though Benjamin may – with the car! Much love and I hope you will get through comfortably.

Your loving Mum.

Pop had started to teach Ben to drive at seventeen years old, as he had with us all. Poor Ben didn't have much chance, as Pop was always being ill and consequently had less patience with him than he had with us. Finally as Ben was not getting on very fast I took over teaching him. He was an apt pupil and soon learnt to drive very well.

The last letters I ever received from my father were dated January 4th 1934, which was his fifty-seventh birthday, and two days later, January 6th.

January 4th:
My beautiful daughter Beth

Thank you so much for all your wishes, I need them very much, my dear . . . . I've just had some of your drink and don't feel any better for it!! I'm not getting up today as I have a temp. – not much, just an excuse . . . . It was so nice having you home; my four are the finest four on earth. Ben is a perfect dear and, of course, Mum is one of God's angels.

Goodbye, my daughter. I can't write much, but I wish you would "do my buttons up".

Goodbye, Beth. Your loving father.
R. V. Britten. Pop.

January 6th 1934
My dear beautiful daughter Beffy

I'm up again after a heavenly day. That "dope" [i.e. morphia] suits me down to the ground, even the sweeezzing! went. Don't I wish I could have it every night . . . . Dr. Wolff was very prompt, wasn't he, with the cheque? I am enclosing mine. It was £20, not £25, wasn't it? . . . . I hope this will really put you on your feet, Beth, and from now on you will pay your way. I hate you having to work at all but I feel it is a good thing, better than a shop.

Goodbye my daughter, my love to thee.

From this moment he became increasingly worse. The doctors gave my mother a definite date for him to die, one of them in January; then, as he lived on, another in February, and still he lived on. We all felt he should see another specialist for no definite diagnosis had as yet been made. As Barbara was in the medical world, she said she would make enquiries about who was the best to have.

March 6th 1934. Lowestoft. Mum writes:

I haven't time to write more than a few words, because I have been making Pop take his tea for about 1½ hours! He had a bad pain this morning in his chest and I had to send for Dr. Evans who, after examining, said he had better take some morphia, so he is happy. He said that if he didn't cough the pain would be better. Will you tell Barbara this and that the "Chest Specialist" is coming tomorrow about 4 o'c. Tell her that I am writing to you tonight and to her after he has been tomorrow night, and if time I will write to you too – if not she will tell you all. Pop is much more hopeful himself than he has been before and I am not going to allow them to do anything to depress him again. You know all this is contrary to my C.S. [Christian Science] but I am only doing as the family wants and Pop himself!

I long for tomorrow evening and for it all to be over . . . Benjamin is in Norwich for his "do". He has just rung up and says that it went moderately well and was received well. Mangeot wasn't pleasant but all is smoothed over it seems. He is coming back with Mrs. Coleman and Charles by 7.45. Caesar sends his love – at least would if he could. Pop is sleeping happily and free from pain.

My fondest love. Your loving Mum.

So on March 7th this famous specialist went to Lowestoft and examined our dear father. On his return to London he wrote the most extraordinary letter to the effect that there was really nothing wrong with Pop, and had better get up and get on with some work. We were stunned. We all thought that his bill for twenty pounds should be ignored. One can only hope for his sake that somehow or other the specialist's notes were mixed with those of another patient.

One month later, on April 6th 1934, our father died. On that very day Mum wrote to me:

> My darling little Beth
>
> How I wish you were here, but I expect you are quite happy and I do hope the Gills are back [the Gills occupied the top flat of our dressmaking premises]. I hate you being alone. Can't you go and stay somewhere for the weekend?
>
> Our dear old "Pop" is about the same, thoroughly under morphia at the moment but only 1½ grains today, and it is having the same effect. He misses his Beth and so do I. I am so glad you are coming next weekend. Think – a week today you will be here and Benjamin too; so will the nurse, so you won't have so much to do, only keep him company while she is out.
>
> Dr. E syringed the opening this morning, so it ought to do good. The pulse and heart are as good as usual. Barbara and Stephen Abell have been putting on the green and again tomorrow. I'm so glad she has, it's good for her and she has a passion for it!
>
> Goodnight my pet – must write a few cards to the aunts.
> Heaps of love and hugs
> Your loving Mum."

(Pop's bed had been moved into the window, so that he had a good view of the harbour and the putting green, and he could watch Barbara putting.)

The death mercifully was caused by a cerebral haemorrhage and not by the lymphadinoma which was the final diagnosis of his disease, which would have meant lingering on in a dreadful state for months. Pop had had thrombosis since the influenza epidemic in 1917, and it is thought that a clot had come adrift in his leg and caused the haemorrhage.

Early on the morning of Saturday, April 7th, I had a telephone call from home asking me to come home but not saying why. I was surprised, as I had planned to go the next weekend and Barbara was at home. They told me when I arrived that Benjamin was on his way home from Florence, where he had won a prize at the International Society of Contemporary Music and his piece *Phantasy Quintet* was being performed there. He was travelling home with a friend, John Pounder. Suddenly, to our horror, we all realized that the announcement of Pop's death had been put in the papers – would Ben by some mischance see this? What a terrible shock it would be for him. Although we had been half expecting father to die for months, somehow when it happened it was horrible. We all loved this marvellous man so much, Ben and I perhaps more than the two older ones. They were out in their worlds with their partners, so home and parents by then did not mean so much to them as they did to us. Ben and John, on their way home, did buy a paper to read, but being young they were not interested in births, marriages and deaths, so they did not see that Pop had died.

Afterwards, we found a letter addressed to the four B's in his drawer, together with some morphia pills which he had hidden. He was so afraid of becoming a burden, I am sure he would have taken them if he had got any worse. The letter simply said:

> Goodbye my four, my love to you all. It's grand to have known you and have your love. Comfort Mum.

Surprisingly, Mum did not collapse after the death, although we felt sure she would, having been so brave and borne the strain of those last years so marvellously. Pop had so hated the idea of going to hospital and she was determined that she would keep him at home. I am sure she made this tremendous effort for our sakes. Mum loved us all, especially her beloved Benjamin, but the chief love of her life had gone. We noticed from then on a general deterioration in her, as she seemed to go slowly downhill until her final illness. The reason for her to go on living seemed to have gone. I could not help recalling those lines of Sir Henry Wotton, in his poem on the *Death of Sir Albert Moreton's Wife*:

> He first deceased, she for a little tried
> To live without him, liked it not, and died.

My cousin Elsie Hockey told me that when she was staying with Mum in Lowestoft soon after Pop died, she noticed that every afternoon about five o'clock Mum disappeared. One day Elsie asked her where she had been.

She replied, "I have been sitting by Robert's grave."

Our mother had several good friends in Lowestoft who were Christian Scientists and they persuaded her to become one. I do not think that she would have done so had she not been so desperately anxious about Pop and ready to clutch at any straw. She still remained a good member of her own church, and thus went along with both faiths.

After our father died the practice was taken over by his partner, Lawrence Sewell, and it was obvious that the Lowestoft house was far too big for our mother to live in alone. One of her Christian Science friends had gone to live in Frinton, an exclusive seaside town in Essex, and persuaded her to go and look at the place to see if she liked it. This she did and decided to go and live there. It had the advantage of being much nearer London than Lowestoft so that Barbara, Ben and I could get there more easily. We all went with her to help find a house and finally we found a little house on top of a cliff overlooking the sea. It was called Biltmore, Pole Barn Lane, in the least smart end of the town. The house is not there any more, it had a direct hit from a doodle bug during the war.

It had a little garden just big enough for Mum to have fun in, and we found a maid called Florence. It would have been unthinkable for Mum, at that time, not to have a living-in maid. Getting the house ready to move into and buying new furniture and furnishings (for the big pieces of furniture had either been sold or left behind) gave Mum a great lift. She loved doing houses and making them pretty. Often at Lowestoft she would have all the furniture moved around to make a change, much to my father's disgust – he thought it all right as it was. She could not move the furniture in the drawing-room too much as there were large holes in the carpet which had to be hidden until finally, when the expense of our education was coming to an end, a beautiful new chinese carpet was bought.

Pop left everything unconditionally to our mother; amounting to £15,000 which, considering that he had had no inherited money and had educated four children, with only Benjamin assisted by grants and scholarships, was a remarkable achievement. We always lived well in a comfortable home, Mum had her servants and nice clothes, Pop had his drinks and books; what hardships we suffered, such as cold bedrooms and cold baths, were not for economy's sake but for character building. The tragedy for Pop was that he was never able to retire from the work that he hated and live in the country, which was always his dream. He also had been wonderfully good to all his in-laws.

10

Travelling Abroad

About this time, October 1934 Benjamin decided to go to Europe to spend the money he had won for travel. Ben thought it would be a good idea for her to go with him. They went first to Basle in Switzerland, where they knew a lot of people who were happy to give them hospitality. Two Swiss girls who had stayed with us in the summer of 1920, Lisel and Bethly, both lived there and through them I had had an exchange with a young friend of theirs, Yvonne Clar so there was all her family as well.

They left England in October 1934. On October 24th my mother writes:

> I promised to write to you after we had seen Yvonne. We went there to dinner at the Casino [Yvonne's parents owned the Casino in Basle] – on Monday and on Tuesday I went to tea at Yvonne's flat to her baby's first birthday party ... These people know how to build and run houses – every convenience. Their food is <u>too</u> much! Of course we are much entertained among them all. Bethly's and Lisel's fathers and mothers, and now we are staying by invitation with Bethly's sister, who has a lovely very modern house, baths and all toilet places perfectly wonderful. You told me all about it when you were here and now I see for myself. We are going to lunch with Mrs Schlotterbeck, so I must go and change my dress and do my hair and finish this afterwards.
>
> ... I expect we are here until Monday or Tuesday for various opera. We heard and saw Rigoletto last night with Bethly who took tickets, and tonight to Bethly to dinner to meet a man and his wife who teach at the Conservatoire and Benj will show him his work. They are trying to get Weingartner to meet Benj. We shall hear today! We are in so little that there is not time for letters or sewing and mending. I am well; Benj has a bad headache but it will go soon. Tomorrow we go to *Magic Flute*, Mrs Schlotterbeck has given us tickets,

and Saturday the Clars [Yvonne's parents] have tickets for a Strauss do at the theatre with Weingartner and Elizabeth Schumann.

(Next day): Benjamin has gone for an interview with Weingartner who will advise us where to go and whom to see. I will tell Barbara in my weekend letter and she will tell you. I can't write very much and I have so many letters to write. Today Bethly's sister-in-law, who has divorced her husband (we met her last time-up in Arosa), has come unexpectedly to lunch. She is delightful and showed me some photos taken when we were up there, one of Pop and it came unexpectedly – I showed my sorrow! but she said you are better off than I am – she loved him! [i.e. her divorced husband]. More when I see you. She drove us up past Dornach. She lives near the Goethe Anum! [Goetheanum] and has a wonderful house in perfect scenery. We had tea in the garden. I can't describe it all, but you know as you have been here yourself and know all about the cars and excursions and rich meals! . . . . . . We are going to *Magic Flute* tonight and Saturday to Weingartner's concert, Strauss; on Sunday afternoon to *Aida*!

Goodnight my darling sweet. I must dress in your lace dress and show off your creation! We expect to go to Vienna on Monday.

Much love from your devoted Mums.

Letter to Barbara from Ben. Hotel Hapsburg, Salzburg. October 30th 1934.

My dearest Barbara,

I am awfully sorry not to have written before this – if only to answer all your numerous letters you have so kindly sent me. It was a pity that they all were lost in the post. I suppose Sloane Square station pillar-box is continually being robbed. Nevertheless – as Mum is writing this morning I thought I would therein put a letter, and save the colossal expense incurred in sending Briefs to England. I suppose that Mum has told you what a gap it leaves in our monies when we post letters – why, it is cheaper to travel first-class to London than to send a letter there – or nearly.

You must forgive any little foreign idioms that occasionally spring into this letter. I have been talking so much German that it is with much effort that I can write in English. My German is nearly as good as your Swiss was – but can you say: "Der Metzger wetzt das Metzgemesser!?"

We had a great time in Basel, as Mum will have you told. I think it is a good place, and the people are too awfully hospitable. They simply wouldn't let us do anything ourselves – they almost wanted to feed us. And the food. Ooh the food, the hors d'oeuvres were so good that I invariably had to stop after it, & see delicious soufflés, Florilla, Bombes glacés, whisked away from our very noses.

I agree with you about the Kauffman-Meyer couple. Flausi only turned up for Saturday & Sunday before we left. But Bethly we saw practically every day. I think she's a saint. Just a saint. And Lisel is an awful dear – her husband and child are most amusing. Peterli is the most rampageous kid ever known – but we got on well together, and he taught me a lot of bad German.

This is a funny place – quite nice in spots. But the sheets are only as wide as the mattress & (tell it not in Gath) there was last night no paper (Sshh!) in the (aunt) –

To resume in loud tones – it will be nice to see the place and see where Mozart was born etc.

Of course the journey yesterday was almost silly it was so lovely – all through the south of Switzerland, and the whole length of the Tyrol.

At first we were springing up all the time & shrieking wildly at each hill – but at the end we were blasé, and murmured – "not a bad glacier over there – what!" But, I have never seen anything like it.

We go to Wien on Thursday, & then duty starts. I shall have to go round introducing myself to crowds of people, who will never have heard of English music (don't blame them), and who don't speak English.

By-the-way, I shall probably have to come back to London for Nov. 30th & come out to Paris for a few weeks after – as I have a first performance at Wigmore Hall, & even if I don't hear the show, I must see that Betty Humby (pianist) plays the pieces properly. So keep the date.

I hope the job is going well, & that you are settling down more. Bethly sent her love, & we all drank your health on Sunday at her flat — in the presence of Bethly, Flausi, Ade Eisinger, Rosemary same, & a friend. I don't think the Reinharts were there. By-the-way, if you can possibly see Kati Eisinger who is staying in London (have you her address) it would be nice – as they were so good to us.

Tell Beth I'll write when Mum writes – as I can't afford the stamp.

Much love

Benjamin

Hotel Regina, Vienna. November 4th 1934

My dear Sissy,

I am so sorry not have written to you before. But each time I write it is as good as a birthday present for you – it's so expensive – if we hadn't been so wise and changed our money before we came to Austria it would have cost us just a 8d for each letter. So you won't have many birthday presents, or Xmas, from me for the next few years. Today I am letting Mum put her letter in with mine, in the hope that she will pay for the stamp.

Well – everything here is going well. We've had marvellous times everywhere so far. The Baselites were all terribly nice to us. Bethly and all her family are saints. I liked Lisel and her husband too; as well as her son. We saw a lot of them too; many meals, and Lisel took us out alot in the car all over the place. Peterli [the son] is a most amusing kid; taught me quite a lot of German. It was nice to see Yvonne again – I think she & Charlie are a nice couple – he certainly is most attractive. I wasn't frightfully smitten with her parents though, although they gave us a super meal at the Casino. There were also a nice English cousin of Charles & his mother there too, I have his London address. Weingartner was very nice, but not much help. He was very busy, & couldn't (or wouldn't) give me the introductions I wanted. But he gave me a ticket for the rehearsal of a show he was conducting, which was interesting. The music in Basle is very good, you know. You must have gone with your ears shut.

I suppose Mum has told you about our journey to Salzburg & on to here. It was very interesting seeing where Mozart was born, wrote and lived & all that sort of thing. It rained on the day we came on here, & today – the only two wet days we've had so far. According to all the papers London has been buried under snow several times. Also I see that someone has flown to or from Australia. Is this true or only an exaggeration?

We went to the opera last night – ooh what a show! Fledermaus, by Johann Strauss, one mass of Viennese Waltzs, marvellously played, sung & danced. We couldn't have had a better introduction to Viennese Opera. Today I went to a concert of the Philharmonic orchestra – a glorious orchestra – never heard one like it before.

The Viennese, from what little we have seen of them – in shops, at concerts, people we've met – are awfully nice & pleasant, except that they don't speak too much English. But my German is lovely now of course.

Mum seems to be better. Gets very dazed and dizzy at times, but that is to be expected considering we are travelling so much, & seeing so many new things. I have to be rather careful with her really, although she is being awfully sweet, & putting nothing in my way. You have heard the new arrangements? – Here for about 16 days more – then Munich for a week – then home for Nov. 30th (beastly curse but it has got to be done); then probably, if I have enough time and money (before Christmas, i.e.) I shall try & come back to Paris for a week or two by myself. If I can't do that I shall either go there after Christmas, or wait until Easter & come here again. This all depends on what money I have left – but it looks as though I shall have a little.

We are staying on here, because it is as cheap as going to the pensions we have seen, & infinitely more comfortable.

I hope things are going well with you – & that more orders have come in. I expect that they will come in after abit, when people begin to think of Christmas. I hope you are well, & Barbara also. Give her my love & tell her I'll write for Xmas, or even before. By-the-way, please don't forget that I shan't be 21 before Dec. 10th or thereabouts!!
Cheerioh, Beth! See you soon. All the best.
Benjamin.

I imagine that he said he would not be twenty-one before December 10th, because he would be away for November 22nd and would want to keep it properly when Mum and he returned.

My mother wrote the same day to me, so that they could share the stamp! November 4th 1934 – she writes:

Thank you for your letter which followed us here. I was glad to have it . . . . Well, here we are in Vienna, and a marvellous place it is, though we haven't seen an awful lot of it yet! We had both decided to go to a Pension from this hotel; and went and looked at one in the city – a *very* noisy place – and at another some distance from here – and the opera – rather stuffy – pleasant woman – English speaking, wanted 11 shillings daily and % I suppose on the bill – and what most places charge! Then we came back here. The manager who had offered to keep us for 12 shillings, and was most anxious to keep us – the Hotel is large and in Frei Plaz – beautiful garden leading into the Ring – the place where every important building is – Opera, Parliament and lovely University besides other places – it is like this with the Danube at one side it takes one hour to walk round it in the gardens. Where was I? Oh – the manager kept coming to us at meal times and say-ing "Sassfied? Yah?!" We, or rather I, had a talk with him and said our rooms were noisy and rather difficult for B. to work in and that we'd been to a Pens. offering us, etc., etc. So he took us and showed us quiet rooms – next to each other – and H&C water, and said *he* would take us for 11 shillings! and cold baths too! So we decided to stay. There is a big restaurant and a little quiet nice one – where we feed. No worry about tips, it's charged on the bill – a good thing too, as there are dozens of waiters. Such kind men really! The food is beyond de-scription. Yesterday we went to a marvellous Opera to hear *The Bat* – Johann Strauss. The house was amazing, big, spacious and brilliantly lit. We paid about 9/-to 10/-, an Austrian schilling is worth about 10d to us. It's all very puzzling, the money.

Salzburg was so interesting, but very little music on. The Mozart Museum and houses where he and his people had lived were very interesting, and we were very happy because the scenery was won-derful, all surrounded by mountains, some in the distance. We saw a funny thing as we came home one evening in Salzburg, a man riding a bicycle ran into another *do.* and knocked him off (he didn't fall off himself). The one on the ground jumped up, ran to the other, pummelled him, hit him with a big box as hard as possible – a verit-able paddy! Shocking exhibition of temper. The assaulted argued and shouted but they both got on their bicycles and rode away! . . . .

Now my sweet, don't write more than once a week, but I'd like to hear once – how things are going. I am going to send you the velvet coat made last year to be altered . . . . I must tell you that Mrs. Clar sent you an invitation to go there anytime – she said it once or twice. Goodnight, my Beth, be good, say your prayers, think of him if you smoke too much! [My father started me smoking, at least I copied everything he did; then he felt very guilty and made a pact with me to smoke only ten a day. He kept to it but I don't think I did.]

Mum continues: "I have a letter from him [meaning Pop] and I'll put at the side what he said: Give my love to our Beth and tell her I expect her to be what all our kids are – 'Perfect'."

They obviously had doubts of me. I never could give up smoking.

*

November 11th 1934, Armistice Day. She writes:

... Today is *your* letter day and although it is the 11th, there is no two minutes' silence. I believe that on Tuesday 13th there is a demonstration by the socialists in memory of the Revolution. I think we shall be careful on that day, but they say it is harmless. Benjamin meant originally to go to St. Stephen's at 9.0 o'c. (R.C. I believe) but we didn't get home until 12 o'c. from *Carmen,* which we went to last night and we were tired, and had dejeuner at 9.45! I am going to the Christian Science Service at 11.35. He won't come with me to stay, but will walk about. He was very tired and felt seedy last night but is all right now! The theatre was very hot – Volksoper they call it, and everywhere is <u>so</u> heated. *Carmen* was wonderful: a singer I believe you heard in Covent Garden with Grace Williams and Benj, took the part of Carmen – Maria Olszewska – magnificent acting and singing. I think reading of other people's pleasures is dull! but I feel I must tell you of our doings. Madame Köller, the CS Practitioner, has been very kind to us. I had occasion to need her help and then asked her to tea. She is perfectly charming, so human too! We were both very taken with her! Well, she shares a box at the opera with four others and they offered B. a seat for one night. I went to a play in German! on Friday at the Burgtheater, a lovely building only a little smaller than the Grand Opera House. Of course, I only understood about ten words, but Madame K. told me the plot and it was easy to follow. This afternoon we are going to Hansel and Gretel; couldn't resist it! as we love it so. It is in the Volksoper and not so good as the other places, but really very good indeed even then – must go now.

83

Later: This afternoon a disappointment for B. Hansel and Gretel was just a sort of pantomime story with a piano! and he left at the beginning. I came home and fetched him out to tea in a cafe because I had no milk – I always make it in the bedroom – but Sunday is an awkward day. It was funny, very full and strange,. We went into the lovely church for a few minutes on our way home, but there was Mass going on. There has been no service in connection with Armistice that I can hear of . . . . . . Benji sends his love; he is rather tired today, trying to think of a title still for those piano pieces . . . . . . Today we start our fifth week. You ask why letters are so expensive to write: they cost about c6 and I think it is the exchange – so that is why I write all I can.

I must write to the insurance people about Benjamin's continuing his payments, so goodnight my Beth. I long to see you again and talk over everything – there is so much to say . . . . .

They could get cold baths, but not hot ones. If any of my readers have travelled in Europe about that time they must have experienced this difficulty. I remember when, at the invitation of Ben and Peter Pears I was staying at Elmau near Munich with my children. I desperately needed a hot bath, because we were skiing. I asked for one, they said "Oh yes, of course", so I got one. It was filled to the brim with boiling water; if I had got in, it would have flowed over. After that, I was allowed to use the one which Ben and Peter had. They had a private bathroom, which they should, as they were performers. Ben and Peter were kindly giving us this wonderful holiday out of the money they would receive from performing at Elmau. Mum, however, was not able easily to get a hot bath, so she washed all over in the hand basin and, while balancing on one leg, she fell and gashed her leg rather badly. She said nothing to Ben about it because she did not want to worry him. She arrived home with a horrid leg and I made her go to see a doctor about it.

I went down to Lowestoft while Mum and Ben were away to see if everything was in order.

*

On November 18th she writes:

Thank you for inspecting our house. I am glad to hear that Florence [the maid] was all she should be and all well with Caesar (the dog) . . . . . . About you and Caesar sticking to the floor! Did it look nice?

A good colour? (I had stained some of the floors). There are parquet floors everywhere we have been, very nice to look at, but very creaky floors, things seem to creak all night. Benj. is out to tea with a friend of Grace Robert and an American who is staying with him. He went to lunch with a man he had an introduction to, so I have yet to hear how he has got on. His German is quite good. I went to the Spanish Riding School today. Lovely horses and stepping so daintily in time to the music: Valse, Gavotte, Polka and Quadrille! I was told I ought to see it. Pop would have loved the horses (not their dancing I think), they were lovely creatures. We had a wonderful time at both the Meistersingers and Siegfried and on Monday night we go to Götterdämmerung, the last at the opera for us. We go in the top gallery or the one below that, so we needn't dress. All the women seem to dress, full or demi-semi, but very few men! I try to see some things to tell you, but the clothes are in much the same fashion as England I think, with women; but the men wear more colours, and so different from our men. Benjamin looks most remarkable in his grey flannel trousers – everyone stares at him! . . . . . . The weather is like spring, only about two chilly days and 1½ rainy! No sign of fog and very little mist. This is a wonderful city. We should like to see it under snow! But no such luck, I fear. We shall go from here on Wednesday early, I expect about 8, unless we travel by night on Tuesday. We have to go to Munich, because of financial reasons too long to explain here. Benj. is well now, but had a sort of 'flu – temp., violent headache and leg pains. Had all Monday in bed and part of Tuesday – and got up for lunch and we went to the opera! It cured him! But I was a bit anxious! Took him there and back in a taxi, not very ruinous here! But five hours of it! We went to a concert rehearsal yesterday afternoon. Exactly like a concert, packed with people, not a seat to spare. They did a Bruckner Symphony and the Tchaikovsky *Pathetic* – very lovely the last; the first Benj. said was very poor music. The Orchestra was wonderful, beyond praise! Now au revoir till tomorrow morning.

I can't find anything to bring for presents. It will have to be just sweets. I don't want to have the customs down on me. I have had to buy some tea and it costs from 12/- to 15/- per lb (English tea – the stuff they give us isn't tea) . . . . . .

My mother loved her tea and wherever she went she always took with her a

85

spirit stove and kettle with which to brew her morning cup and afternoon tea.

They flew home from Paris and I met them at Croydon. My mother was very proud of herself, as it was quite an adventure in those days.

While they were abroad I was flat hunting. Ben wanted something better than the boarding house to live in, and I was sick of my bed-sitter. I found a small one in West Hampstead which was cheap, it had two bedrooms, a sitting room, bathroom and kitchen. The only snag we found later was the cold. It was over the entrance to a garage, and consequently had concrete floors and nothing but air all around it.

It was fun furnishing it and setting up our first home. The only thing we needed now was a car, there had been a car in the family ever since either of us could remember. The Humber Super Snipe my father had bought when he was ill had to be sold as it was too expensive for us to run. We went to a car auction and Ben bought a two-seater Lagonda 1924 for £5. The previous owner had tried to make it look more modern by cutting the hood off and lowering it. The trouble with that was that it rubbed on ones head and when it rained it leaked. We had a very funny journey back from Frinton one pouring wet day. We had taken some sticking plaster with us and when we thought we had located the leak we stuck a bit on the hood. The car would always go down to Frinton but never wanted to come back. One day Ben was coming back alone, he stopped to relieve himself behind a hedge and when he tried to start the car again the starter came out in his hand. In those days there was no key starter it was just a knob that you pulled.

11

Starting to Earn a Living as a Composer

In the year after leaving the College, Ben had made some progress earning his living as a composer. He had been fortunate in his contact with the Macnaghten-Lemare concerts of new music at the Ballet Club Theatre (later known as the Mercury Theatre) at Notting Hill Gate. Many of his works were performed there, such as the *Phantasy for String Quintet* and *Three Two-Part Songs for female voices* to words by Walter de la Mare. The critics were mostly very unkind to him, dismissing him as 'clever', eclectic, and unfavourably comparing him with Walton, Vaughan Williams, etc. In fact he had little encouragement from the critics during his life, particularly at his first appearance on the musical scene. He said to me late in life: "The critics don't like me". He gave up reading them.

I always went with Ben to the concerts at the Notting Hill Gate Theatre and it was fascinating to see the young composers there. Ben was by far the youngest of them all. Edmund Rubbra would stride about with his long hair flying out behind him, which was remarkable for people did not wear long hair then. Elisabeth Lutyens and Elizabeth Maconchy often had new works performed there.

In early 1935 a very fortunate thing happened for Ben. Edward Clark, who was working on documentary films for the G.P.O., contacted him and asked him to write music for these films. Clark had already collected some remarkably talented people, such as Wystan Auden, Bill Coldstream (later Sir William), Louis MacNeice, Christopher Isherwood. This at last put Ben in touch with the intellectuals of his generation, although he was much younger than any of them. Wystan Auden was nearly ten years older; and had been at Gresham's some years before Ben. Ben said that working for the Film Unit was wonderful training, because he had to work quickly to order, and force himself to work when he did not want to. There was not enough money to buy the special sound effects needed, so they had to improvise with the material to hand. One day Ben related to me that they had been making a most horrible mess in the studio. They were filming *The Herring Fleet* and trying to make the sound of a ship unloading in the dock. They had pails of water sloshing around, drain pipes with coal sliding down them, tin whistles, etc. He had enjoyed himself and had achieved the sounds he wanted.

These early experiments stood him in good stead in his future works. He became a past master of getting the sounds he needed out of all sorts of strange things. Another thing he had to learn with the G.P.O. Film Unit was to write scores for six or seven instruments.

While Ben was working for the Unit, he was given a commission to write the music for a feature film, *Love from a Stranger* (Trafalgar Films), directed by Rowland V. Lee, with Basil Rathbone and Ann Harding as the stars. This was a very frustrating time. He was kept hanging about for weeks at the studio, then he would be asked to write something, but by the time it was done the director had changed his mind and it would be scrapped. After some weeks he was told the music must be finished by a certain date, with four days in which to write it. Poor Ben, he worked through the nights, on and on. I longed to be able to do something to help him, but I could only make him coffee and make sympathetic noises. He finished the music in time, but it also finished his ever wanting to write for feature films again. In fact, although he was asked constantly to do so, he never would. The only film he said he would compose the music for, would be if any of Arthur Ransome's books were made into a film. There was a plan to make one later and Arthur Ransome approached Ben about the music, but the film was never made.

During 1935, Ben and I were both happy living in our funny little flat. We were both very occupied with our work but we went away for most weekends, usually together, either to Frinton to see our mother – we tried not to let a weekend go past without a visit from one of us – or to stay with the Bridges at Friston, or to one or other of our aunts. We loved to stay with Aunt Flo at Whiteshill in Gloucestershire and to walk in the lovely country. Our little car went happily up and down the very steep hills. The buses going from Stroud to Whiteshill had spikes at the back in case the brakes should give way. On one occasion we arrived to find Aunt Flo trying to drown the kittens of Smutty (the white cat) in a bucket of water; they were swimming round and round in the bucket. We were horrified and immediately filled the bucket to the brim and put a piece of wood over it to remove any air. Aunt Flo became very much an eccentric old maid, she had always been slightly odd but became more so as she grew older, and she became increasingly mean.

We tried to stay with her in summer rather than winter, because, in spite of being brought up in Lowestoft in hardy conditions, even Ben and I felt the cold there was a bit too much. Flo lived until she was well over eighty, so the stark living conditions cannot have harmed her too much. She had a very kind heart and would have given us anything if she felt we really needed it. We both loved her dearly.

On July 4th 1935, Basil Wright drove Benjamin down to Colwell near Malvern, where Wystan Auden was a master at a boys' preparatory school. Ben had been commissioned to write the music for the scripts of two films *Coal Face* and *Night Mail,* and Wystan had been engaged to write the scripts, so it was necessary that the two should meet.

It was understandable that Ben should admire and be influenced by Wystan. He had never met anyone like him before. Wystan Auden was sophisticated, brilliant, amusing and, above all, a great poet, a master of words, and he taught Benjamin much about the English language and about poetry. Treating words and poetry was to become his greatest quality in music. He told me that he considered Wystan to have a first class brain, but I said loyally "What about you?", for I could not believe anyone to be better than Benjamin. He replied "Oh, my brain is only second class".

Wystan in 1935 had started to write in collaboration with Christopher Isherwood, his first full length play *The Dog beneath the Skin,* or *Where is Francis?* Ben took me to the first performance of this play, which was performed by the Group at the Westminster Theatre in January 1936.

About this time Ben also got to know the writer John Pudney. John had also been at Gresham's School, but long before Ben. In *Britten – A formative recollection,* which was printed in the programme of a concert given by the New Philharmonia Orchestra as a Tribute to Benjamin Britten in the Royal Festival Hall on February 22nd, 1977, he writes of the circumstances of their meeting:

> I was a junior BBC sound radio producer on loan from London to North Region with the task of doing a programme from Newcastle about Hadrians Wall. The BBC did not go much for outside talent in those days. I was not popular in insisting on commissioning Auden to write the programme.
>
> It contained chorus songs for the Roman Garrison and incidental music for a small orchestra. "Let's bring in Benjy" Auden said on the telephone.

"But we have a man who does this sort of thing" Manchester BBC told me.

We stuck out for our Mr. Britten.

"But he's so young and he has only had one thing broadcast, London says".

Auden threatened strike action. I was young enough to do battle. We won. "It's not terribly important but it is irregular". Manchester conceded. "And who will you get to conduct the chorus of Northumbrian miners and the orchestra that have been booked?"

"Mr. Britten is coming up for rehearsals and transmission" I told them.

"Glad I'm not in your shoes. Just wait till those miners and the Newcastle orchestra come face to face with a boy from the south with a load of manuscript . . ."

My joyous memory is of that curly-haired smiling slender youth modestly entering the studios, of people being taken aback, of a few contemptuous murmurs – then suddenly of Benjamin taking command, the miners singing like Romans with sparkling eyes, the little orchestra hard pressed with the unfamiliar score but grinning.

And of course one of the basses said "He'll go a long way, that lad."

Recordings were not made of minor programmes like that. Whether the words and music have survived I have never discovered. The memory is bright.

I recollect very well Ben's writing the music for that programme, his going up North and coming back thrilled with that part of the country and particularly Hadrian's Wall. He had not realised before what a wonder it was. He told me he got on well with the miners' chorus and that they sang his piece like Trojans.

Until the end of 1935 the Oxford University Press had taken on the very few works of Ben's that had been published, but now Ralph Hawkes, of Boosey and Hawkes, came up with a proposition. He offered Benjamin a contract by which Boosey and Hawkes would pay him a sum annually, £150 to start with. They would publish everything they thought fit, but would be his sole publishers. At the beginning obviously they would lose money, but they had the foresight to see that they were on to a good thing. This was in itself surprising, for until then Boosey and Hawkes had only gone in for light music, jazz, etc. Ben signed the contract, and later the amount was raised to £400, as his music became better known. Ralph Hawkes became a good friend and adviser to Ben, and remained so until his tragic early death in 1950.

In the summer of 1979 I went to see Sophie Wyss, the singer, who had known and worked with Ben at this time. She was over eighty and still living at 19 The Mall, Surbiton, where she had lived with her husband Arnold Gyde the publisher and their young sons, and where Ben and I had often visited the Gyde family. The house had changed very little. Arnold senior was dead, but Sophie was still her charming self with the beautiful speaking voice and French accent. Her sight was going but she was looking after herself entirely. Sophie was very happy to talk about Benjamin and the past. She spoke about the new works she was asked to sing:

> "One works hard for weeks, one sings the work once and very often never sings it again. It is the end, a stone thrown into the water, leaving scarcely a ripple. Not so with Benjamin Britten. In his case it was not a stone but bread cast on the water. He was a student at the Royal College when I first met him. A boy with crisp curly fair hair, a pale expressive face, often lit by a charming laugh. He really seemed as if he were from the Olympian land of Pan and Syrinx (I had just been singing about them!) He never seemed to have to learn anything, he knew it all by instinct. He played piano accompaniments with the ease and grace of someone who had given a lifetime to the piano. He knew what little effects could be conjured from each instrument. We would work away together at my house, Benjamin urging me on to do the almost impossible; then he would go out to play cricket with my ten-year-old son. We would all dine together and he would talk with bitter humour about the way the world was drifting to war. Then he would telephone with frenzied energy to one of his circle of friends – already a formidable circle it was too: W. H. Auden, Christopher Isherwood, Louis MacNeice, Stephen Spender, Lennox Berkeley.
>
> He composed 'Our Hunting Fathers', a symphonic cycle for Soprano and Orchestra, to old verses collected and modernised by Auden. It was commissioned by the Norwich Triennial Festival for 1936 and is dedicated to Ralph Hawkes, as loyal a publisher a composer ever had.
>
> My second son was born just in time for me to sing it. The doctor

had forbidden me to sing for several weeks, so my husband and I met Benjamin with his mother and sister Beth in a lovely little Cornish village [Crantock] and there every morning we met in the village hall and Benjamin played *and* sang *Our Hunting Fathers* to me, so that when I was able to resume my singing half of the work was already done.

We had the first rehearsal with orchestra in the loft at Covent Garden. The members of the orchestra were not used to that kind of music and played about disgracefully. When the reference to rats came in the score they ran about pretending they were chasing rats on the floor! They kept asking to leave the room, one after another. It was quite impossible to rehearse at all, the rehearsal broke up in disorder. Poor Benjamin, it was a terrible experience for him, there did not seem to be a chance of a performance at all in Norwich. However, someone must have knocked some sense into them for on the day in Norwich the wretches rallied round and tackled the nimble complexities of the score with good spirit and fair success.

It was a mixed reception from the audience and the critics. It was not an easy or comfortable work to listen to and, being anti-hunting, was not acceptable to many people."

When Ben was asked to write a piece for the 1936 Norwich Festival, he asked Wystan to devise a libretto for him. Wystan chose man's relation to animals as his subject. Not a very wise choice for a new piece by a young composer trying to make a name in the musical world, but Wystan was young and a rebel, and had no thought of bothering about the opinions of a class he despised.

Sophie Wyss continued her reminiscence . . .

"Benjamin had been staying with the Audens in Birmingham and Wystan had been inspiring him with Rimbaud's verse. I met the train at Watford and we travelled together to London. We were separated in the train as it was full. Suddenly Benjamin appeared at my side with great excitement, his eyes shining, and trembling with emotion. He said, 'There is something I must write soon, to some of Rimbaud's poems.'

He did and soon, for voice and string orchestra. The first two, *Being Beauteous* and *Marine*, we did at a concert given by Jan Hoeck in

Birmingham. They were repeated at a 'Prom' in August 1939. Benjamin was already in America by then. A few months later in the States he finished the work, ten poems in all. I did the preliminary work with Franz Reisenstein and I had a wonderful letter from Ben as a guide . . . The first public performance I gave with Boyd Neel in London in 1940. We had a great reception and what Ernest Newman had wittily called 'The Battle of Britten' was won!"

On October 19th 1939 Ben had written to me:

> . . . Wystan & my opera is settled for Broadway <u>when</u> we have done it. We'll have our work cut out doing it, I feel! I've also completed the rest of the '<u>Illuminations</u>' for Sophie to do in November – somewhere in London I believe, but I thought concerts were stopped? Ask Ralph when because I should love you to hear them – they're my best so far.

I did go to hear them and they made a great impression on me.

When Ben and Peter Pears returned from the States in 1942, Ben wanted Peter to sing *Les Illuminations*. This caused a rift between the Gydes and Benjamin. Arnold Gyde was furious and thought Sophie should have sung it. Sophie told me that she would rather have remained friends with Ben and did not mind too much, but her husband could not forgive the slight he felt Sophie had received.

12

Holidays on the Norfolk Broads and in Cornwall

In 1934 and 1935 Ben and I spent two summer holidays on the Norfolk Broads. The first year, at Potter Heigham, we hired an ancient house-boat called "The Ark" and an old sailing boat. There were six of us altogether, three boys and three girls. None of us knew anything about sailing but we had enormous fun exploring the Broads, walking into Heigham to buy stores, falling in and out of the water. The next year we were a bit grander and we hired a bungalow at Thurn, right on the water, and two boats. One was "The Puddleduck", she was built like a tub and was unsinkable. The other boat was a sailing dinghy, which was more fun to sail. A school friend of mine, Gwenllian Rice, and her young brother Edward were with us that time. Ben and Edward shared a tent and Edward was overcome with astonishment when he saw Ben read-ing miniature music scores in bed at night, with apparent enjoyment. He found the simple life and the marshes and birds on the Broads were a congenial place for him. In the Spring of 1936 Ben's *Suite for Violin and Piano* was played by him and Antonio Brosa at the International Society for Contemporary Music in Barcelona. Lennox Berkeley was also having a work performed there, and Benjamin met Lennox for the first time. He felt he needed to go away somewhere by himself and have time to think and write. He met Ethel Nettleship, who had a bungalow and some huts which she let, on a field at Crantock near Newquay, Cornwall. So Ben arranged to hire one of the huts for July and to take over the bungalow for the month of August, when Mum and Robert and Marjorie (Robert's wife) and I would join him.

Ethel and Ursula Nettleship were sisters-in-law of Augustus John, their sister Ida having married him. After bearing him six sons and looking after his mistresses while they were producing his children, Ida died after the birth of her youngest, Henry. Ethel and Ursula brought up Henry; he stayed frequently with Ethel at Crantock, and spent his time swimming and getting to know the Cornish coast. One day in the summer of 1935 Henry had gone off to swim taking his dog with him, but after some hours had not returned, so Ethel went to look for him. All she found was the dog sitting at the top of the cliff and Henry's clothes in a pile beside the dog. They never recovered the body. No one could understand what could have happened, because Henry was such a strong swimmer and knew all about that treacherous coast. It was presumed that he must have had cramp. In the bays on the North Cornish coast there were strong tides and undertows and there were frequent drowning accidents, but these mostly happened to people who could not swim and went too far out. Ben refers to this tragedy in a letter, dated July 9, 1936:

July 9th 1936

Quarryfield
Crantock
Newquay, Cornwall.

My dear Beth,

I hope you got my card announcing my arrival the other day. I am sorry I didn't write yesterday but I had to write to Mum & the Bridges & there didn't seem much time besides.

The journey down was very thrilling. The Cornish Riviera is a terrific train and extremely rapid. I had some difficulty in meeting her Nettleship at the station as I had been told the wrong time of arrival & had to wait for her to turn up. She is somewhat strange and unconventional – but as you might gather from her letters. But she is very kind, not that I see very much of her, though.

The place is very lovely – and beautifully quiet. You can see lots of houses from my window but they are miles across a valley. The coast is very rocky & tempestuous and just as one imagines it to be. Considering all the frightful stories one hears about tragedies in the sea (Miss N. lost a nephew last year – Augustus John's son – here) I don't feel inclined to bathe in a hurry. But the weather has been foul so far – beastly rain all yesterday & a nasty wind to-day – so there hasn't been much temptation.

My woman who is "doing" for me is very nice & quite a good cook – but it is not going to be exactly cheap – £1 per week for hut, 12/6 for woman, & goodness knows what for food & infinite extras. However I expect I shall manage somehow – but don't send me lots of enormous bills for the Lagonda, will you!

Let me have a card saying how you got back from Lewis' etc. I was very worried about you, inspite of the fact you drove so beautifully to Paddington for me! I should use it alot about town if you want to. Saves fares.

I am enjoying myself alot here really. It is lovely to be able to work with absolutely no interruptions. I have alot of good books & lots of lovely walks. But I daresay after a month I shall be pleased to see you.

I must take this to post. Love to Barbara when you see her, & Kathleen. I hope she gets a job. Isn't it good about Mum letting Biltmore for two weeks? Any luck about your flat yet? Perhaps when the summer's over –

Much love,
Benjamin

Ben told me later when we arrived that he had felt sure that Henry John's ghost had sometimes visited him in his hut at night. Henry had slept in that hut before he was drowned. As often as Ben shut the door of the hut, it would swing open again, even on a perfectly quiet still night, with a swish like a sigh.

I used the Lagonda, as Ben had suggested, to drive in London. However, I had an argument with a taxi in the Marylebone Road where traffic lights had only recently come into use. I passed a bus which I thought had stopped at a bus stop and, sailing happily round it, I met a taxi coming from the other side. Traffic lights which had been completely obscured by the bus were against me. It was a very slight accident and we were both able to drive away, but the taxi driver was very nasty about it and called the police. Shortly after this I drove Robert to Cornwall, unaware that a summons had been pushed under the door mat at the flat. There was no letter box in our front door, so all our letters were pushed under the door and the summons had gone to rest under the mat. When Ben and I returned to the flat at the end of August I found that I had been had up for contempt of court and was due to attend the Court the next day. Benjamin said he would come with me. Although I explained to the Judge that the reason I had not attended the previous summons was that it was hidden under the door mat, I was fined £10, to be paid before I left the Court, or go to prison. Of course I did not have that kind of money on me, nor had Ben, but he said not to worry, he would go and get it. So off he went while I waited in the courthouse. Very soon he returned with £10 and released me. I was disqualified from driving for a month, so perhaps it was a good thing I did not get the first summons – I could not have taken the Lagonda to Cornwall.

When Ben asked in his letter "Any luck about your flat yet?", he meant, what chance was there of the flat over our dressmaking establishment becoming vacant? We were both getting tired of the one at West Hampstead and did not want to spend another winter there. Mum had let "Biltmore", our house at Frinton, for two weeks in August, so we were able to hire the bungalow at Crantock on the proceeds. Ben gave up his hut and moved into the bungalow with Mum and Robert, Marjorie, their small son, John, and me. It was a strange assortment of people in cramped conditions.

Ethel Nettleship, the lace maker, was in one of her huts while we were in the bungalow, with their old nurse Katie, and Henry's dog. We had not met Ursula the musician as yet, but were told she would be coming. Ethel and Ursula took it in turns to look after Katie, which was quite a problem as she had become senile and moaned all the time. As they said, she had looked after them when they were growing up (their mother had died when the three girls were children), and they felt duty bound to look after her in her old age. It was the strangest thing to see the procession going to the sea when Ethel went bathing: Ethel in front, then some way behind came moaning Katie, then Henry's dog, even farther behind. When they reached the water's edge, Ethel took off her clothes and lay spread-eagled in the water face down; she had long fair hair which floated out round her. A casual observer would have thought she was drowning. While Ethel was thus floating, Katie and the dog stood at the edge of the sea, Katie and dog moaning and howling respectively. We had been warned that the two sisters had tremendous rows when they were together but did not really believe it. One day over the cliffs strode the strangest figure, singing at the top of her voice. With hair flying and hung around with haversacks, kettles, saucepans, etc. Ursula Nettleship had arrived. What we had been told about the sisters' rows was true. They shared a tent, as the huts were all let, and saucepans, kettles even food flew about inside, sometimes overflowing outside; meanwhile poor Katie, terrified and worried at her two loved ones fighting, stood outside moaning. Fortunately Ursula did not stay long, but went on her way walking along the coast.

We did not get to know her well until later, when Ben asked her to come to Aldeburgh and train the Aldeburgh Festival Choir. She was a marvellous teacher of singing and travelled all over the country, training choirs of all sorts, mostly at Women's Institutes. She was a very natural, lovable person. She built herself a house on the Thames Embankment in Chelsea, where she took in many musicians in need of help and encouragement. There she created a wild garden, for although Ursula would have loved to garden, she had no time for such things. Every time anyone gave her flowers, when they died she threw them outside on her tiny patch to seed. She took up skiing when she was over forty and went each year to Austria. Sadly, during one of the Aldeburgh Festival's "Music on the Meare" events, she slipped getting out of a boat and broke her hip. Soon after she had been allowed for the first time to put her foot to the ground, a young nurse somehow mishandled her and she broke the hip again. She was lame for the rest of her life and had to be on crutches, but nothing daunted that great spirit and she kept on with her teaching with the help of her many marvellous friends. When, over eighty, she died, her friends collected enough money to give in her memory a bridge over a dyke outside the Concert Hall at Snape.

In the autumn of 1936 the upper part of 559 Finchley Road became vacant and Benjamin and I moved into it. We took in a lodger, Kathleen Mead, the daughter of a Lowestoft doctor, to help with expenses, as neither of us was earning much. Mum furnished one of the rooms so that she could come and stay with us whenever she wanted to. We both wanted her to feel free to come, because she was pining on her own at Frinton, but would never have admitted that she was lonely.

Ben was still working with the G P O Film Unit and was very much involved with Wystan Auden, who was a frequent guest at Finchley Road and in Frinton. Both Mum and I liked to have him to stay, he had such beautiful manners. Wystan said to me that it cost nothing to be polite and made life so much more pleasant. He did not suffer fools gladly, but if they were not pretentious, Wystan could be a charming and entertaining companion. However, my housekeeping costs went up considerably whenever Wystan was staying with us as he had an enormous appetite. He also liked to go to bed early after a very hot bath. He had married Erika Mann, daughter of Thomas Mann the German novelist, whom Wystan much admired. Erika in 1937–8 was compering an anti-Nazi cabaret which was having an enormous success in Europe in the countries not already overrun by the Nazis. It was brilliantly written, mostly by the Mann family, father, son and daughter. The Nazis urgently wanted to get hold of the people concerned and put a stop to the cabaret, and the only way this could be avoided was for them to acquire British or American passports. Their problem came to the ears of Wystan Auden and, knowing that he would never want to marry, he agreed to marry Erika by proxy. In any case they could always get divorced later if necessary and this marriage gave Erika the protection of a British passport. When war broke out in Europe with Britain and France, she had to leave and went to the United States of America, where she met her husband for the first time. They did not live together nor did they get divorced, but had an amicable relationship.

Wystan hated London, preferring Birmingham, where he said one could go to bed, which was impossible in London. I remember on one occasion we went to the Café Royal in Piccadilly Circus to have a drink after a concert. When the waiter came to take our order Wystan said he wanted cocoa. I do not think the waiter had ever heard of cocoa, at any rate he did not look as though he had, and Wystan did not get his cocoa. I do not remember what he had, probably nothing.

In the early 30s, Benjamin had met Mary and Bow Behrend, patrons of the arts, at a concert of contemporary music in London. They were impressed by the work of this unknown composer and they asked to meet him. They told him they had a house in the country in Hampshire and invited him to go and stay with them. This he did and so began a friendship which lasted until their deaths. Mary and Bow were very rich (their money was in cotton) but in the nicest possible way. They filled their beautiful home, The Grey House, Burghclere, near Newbury, with struggling young painters, writers, musicians. They rescued Stanley Spencer from the garret in which he was starving and commissioned paintings from him; also Henry Lamb and many others. With them, Ben met many interesting people, including Peter Pears and Peter Burra, a young friend of Peter's. I was fortunate enough to be included in some of these visits. Mary and Bow were kindness itself and did their best to put one at one's ease. Long before private swimming pools became the usual thing, the Behrends had one at the bottom of their garden; it was blue, and the water came out of a copper fish head. To walk through the beautiful garden in the early morning and swim there was such joy, especially coming from the heat of London. Mary and Bow always got up very early to pick flowers for their departing guests to take away with them. Ben enjoyed staying at The Grey House, the stimulating company, the house full of artistic treasures and the chance to swim in the pool which, if not the sea, was the next best thing for one who had a passion for water.

In 1936 the Behrends gave a reception in a house off Park Lane in London. Among other artists, Ben was to play and Sophie Wyss to sing some of Ben's songs. Wystan was staying with us in Finchley Road. He was never bothered about what he wore, but for this occasion he made an attempt to dress correctly. He had no dinner jacket, so he borrowed one which was much too small. He looked so strange, with his tall stooping figure (he stooped, being so short-sighted, with too-short sleeves and trousers). However, he had made the effort to observe the conventions. Not so Stanley Spencer. When the party was in full swing, in came a little man in a shabby brown suit. I thought he must have come to bring more food or glasses, but someone said "There is Stanley Spencer, the painter". Benjamin looked very good in his father's tails, which fitted him well.

Life went on happily for us both in the upper part of 559 Finchley Road, Benjamin working hard on various new works, ideas pouring out of him so fast that he could hardly get them on paper fast enough. During the autumn of 1937 he wrote the first of his song cycles *On this Island*. He chose five lyrics by Wystan, four taken from *Look, Stranger* and *Nocturne* from *The Dog beneath the Skin*. It was a sociable life; with Wystan staying with us and many interesting people came for meals. Christopher Isherwood was a frequent visitor. He must have been at least thirty then, but he looked about fourteen and he would come shyly in at the door and stand on one leg. He still looked very boyish, from the last pictures I saw of him.

13

Illness, and Mother's Death

In January 1937 disaster struck us. Our lodger, Kathleen Mead, a doctor's daughter, got 'flu and gave it to me. After I had looked after her, she went home to Lowestoft to convalesce. I must have been in a low state for I developed pneumonia. I felt very ill and I remember taking my temperature. The thermometer went up and up and when it passed 105 I called Ben, who was fortunately downstairs working. We decided he had better try to find a doctor. He rang Lowestoft and asked our lodger if she could come back and help but her father the doctor would not let her come. Ben, desperate, felt he could not manage on his own. I was very ill by that time, so he rang Mum and she came at once. He also found across the road, at the corner of Platts Lane, a Doctor Moberly, who proved to be a wonderful help and friend. Mum had only been with us for two days when she went down with the bug as well. She developed bronchial pneumonia and I had lumbar pneumonia. At this point Barbara was called on to help and the place became like a hospital with night and day nurses. I never saw my mother again, for we were both too ill to get out of our beds. Then Ben said he felt ill. Barbara, mad with anxiety and worry, said to him: "If you get it, you will have to go to hospital: we cannot nurse anyone else here!", but the day nurse who was looking after Mum and me gave Ben two Dovers Pills which had a severe laxative effect on the poor boy, but he recovered. Christian Scientists were busy working on my recovery, but neglecting Mum. She was not as ill as I was, but in her case she had no will to live; in my case I had just become engaged to be married and life was sweet. My intended, Kit Welford, was then a medical student at St Thomas' Hospital in London so was in touch with the top physicians of the day. Maurice Cassidy kindly came to visit us when he was told of our severe illness. He told the members of the family who were well that while there was life there was hope, adding that there was a new drug which was untried but it might be worth trying it on us. This was almost the first time the M & B, the sulpha drug, had been used; and was probably the reason for my recovery.

My partner Lilian Wolff, as she was then (now Beauchemin) was valiantly carrying on with the dressmaking business downstairs. She now lives on one of the Gulf Islands off Vancouver. I wrote and asked her if she remembered anything special about this time. She answered: "All I remember when you were so ill was the tremendous concern for you of Kit [my fiancé]. It seemed I had more contact with him than Ben or your mother. Ben was for ever racing up that long flight of stairs and, as he was so close to you, I hated to stop and challenge him on your health. There was so much activity and so much concern, and I presume that was why your mother died, the strain must have been very hard on her, but all the attention was over you. My memory of those days is full of small incidents, the tennis at which Ben excelled, the long walks with your father, Ben and the dog across the Southwold Marshes. The tenderness your father showed your mother in escorting her downstairs to the dining-room. Meeting Auden and being awed, etc. etc., and of course always the closeness between you and Ben . . . . . Will look forward to seeing you this summer, hope you can make it. Fond love, as always Lilian."

Barbara was working at her Health Visitor job, but a friend of hers with a car drove her up to Finchley Road each morning early so that she could see to the state of things. There was no room for her to stay, as she had sent for Aunt Effie to cook and look after the household but Barbara spent the weekends with us. She told me that one Sunday, when things were as desperate as they could be and she was relying on the char coming in to help, she did not turn up till late. She had been to church praying for us, she said. Barbara said she felt it would have been more help if she had come to us and prayed another time! In the meantime Kit was being sick – he was always sick if upset about anything.

My mother died and the mourning family went to Lowestoft with the coffin, not knowing whether I would be alive when they returned. They had not dared to tell me she was dead. It must have been terrible for Ben especially, when I asked him how she was, to have to pretend she was better, when all the time she was lying dead in the next room. They must have made a sad group at Lowestoft, but the friends at Lowestoft were marvellous to them. The Nicholson family put them up and looked after them all. Barbara had to stay on to see to things, but Ben returned to London the day after the funeral to see how I was, and I was getting better. I think he told me then that Mum had died. We clung together, for we were the two who loved our parents the most and had been with them much more in the last years. The extra tragedy was that his mother and father did not live to see what their son was to become and were never to hear the wonderful music that he wrote later. It was a pity too that Mum did not have the satisfaction of knowing about all the honours that were heaped on him.

Frank and Ethel Bridge, who had been so very concerned about us and our tragedy, persuaded Ben to take me down to them at Friston Field, which he did as soon as I was strong enough.

We both loved Ethel and Frank dearly, but sometimes wished that Frank would not telephone Ben quite so often in London. Our evenings were frequently interrupted by his lengthy phone calls, he sometimes talked for half an hour. I would have a meal waiting perhaps or someone would be waiting to see Ben. If I went into the sitting room to see if they had finished, Ben would shake his head despairingly; he was much too polite to break off. Frank was a great talker!

Barbara and Robert were executors of Mum's will. I could never understand why she did that. It would have been much better to have made Benjamin one, he always had a good business head. They insisted that the Frinton house should be sold. I pleaded with them to wait a while; as we only had the Finchley Road place, not a proper home, but it was sold, at a loss. A list was made of everything and we chose in turn, starting with the eldest. When we came to the books Ben said it was not fair to start again with the eldest, so he started first to choose the books. Brother Robert came off best with the furniture; he and Marjorie had a large empty school, Barbara had a fully furnished flat which she shared with Helen Hurst, and it was full of Helen's furniture and Ben and I were virtually homeless. Even so, we were too miserable to mind about anything.

The Welfords had become used to the fact that Kit and I were to be married and became fond of Ben and me. They were marvellously kind to us both and stored our furniture at their large place, Peasenhall Hall in Suffolk. When we finally gave up the Finchley Road place in the autumn of 1937, their home became our base. Ben could go when he liked and bring whom he liked to stay there. He had become friends with Peter Pears by then and often Peter came to stay at Peasenhall. I know they loved having Ben there, he was so socially easy. There was not a happy relationship with their sons, and I am sure having us there made things easier. My mother-in-law to be was a stickler for etiquette and liked things on the grand side. There was always a dressing gong for dinner at 7.0p.m. and a gong five minutes before the lunch gong. Woe betide any of us who were late. It seems now that we were all afraid of my mother-in-law. Not so Peter. I remember once when he was staying at Peasenhall he was doing a jigsaw puzzle when the get-ready-for-lunch gong sounded. He did not move and we all said "Peter, didn't you hear the bell?" "Yes I did", he replied, and still did not move. We thought there would be a row, but nothing happened when he strolled late into the dining room.

The Lagonda car finally came to the end of her life, and fetched £2.10.0. In the summer of 1937 Ben bought an A C, a very smart car which does not exist any more. Ben paid £60 for her, which was quite a lot for a second-hand car in those days. He wanted to try her out on a long run, so we decided to go to stay with Aunt Flo in Whiteshill and try the car up and down the steep hills in Gloucestershire. On the way home we were taking turns to drive. I was driving as we approached Maidenhead and Ben wanted to take over. I had a premonition that something was going to happen and did not want Ben to drive, but he insisted, which was very unlike him. The feeling of foreboding was so strong that I sat and waited for whatever it was going to be. There was a lorry in front of us and Ben was about to overtake it. I demurred. The road was fairly straight but rather narrow and I did not think he could see well enough ahead. As we were passing the lorry a car came from the opposite direction. There would have been enough room, but at that moment another car shot out from the approaching car and "WANG", there were cars all over the place. I was out on the road, I cannot think why I was not killed. Ben was all right, but shaken, and his precious new car was a write-off. The only real casualty was a Judge in the first car coming towards us, who at the moment of impact was leaning down to get something off the floor of the car. He got a bang on the head, but fortunately recovered. I was cut about but we were able to get to Aunt Nellie at the Britten family home, the Crescent. This was the only accident Ben had in his life, and he became a first-class driver, and, although in his younger days, liked to drive very fast, he was safe.

After this, Ben bought a second-hand Morris 8 open tourer. He always had to have an open car. The little Morris was a fantastic car. We had her all through the war, until after *Peter Grimes* Ben was a bit richer and started on the idea of buying old Rolls Royces.

14

The Old Mill at Snape

After the house in Frinton was given up, we thought of giving up 559 Finchley Road. I was going to be married and Lilian did not want to carry on alone; she was also practically engaged to be married as well. Ben felt he wanted a home of his own and of course it had to be in Suffolk near the coast. As we were based at Peasenhall Hall, he started to look for something to buy in that area, and finally settled on the wind mill at Snape, a village five miles from the coast, with the river Alde dividing Snape from Tunstall and the marshes. The Mill was still working, though the sails had gone some time ago and an engine had replaced them, but the miller wanted to retire and live somewhere else. In the autumn of 1937, Benjamin bought it for a few hundred pounds and decided to convert the existing buildings, which consisted of the miller's cottage, the granary and the Mill itself, which was a post-mill – a round brick building with a wooden structure supporting the sails, which turned with the wind, so working the grinders.

My future father-in-law, Arthur Welford, was an architect and said he would do the conversion for nothing, which was a great help as Ben had only the £3,000 left him by his mother to spend on the building. The plan was to join the mill to the cottage with a single-storey building which would contain bathroom, shower, boiler house for the central heating and cupboards for linen, etc. The Mill would become Ben's studio and bedroom. To make it possible to have a bedroom above the studio the roof of the Mill had to be raised several feet. From the Mill there was a fantastic view to the south across to the river and the marshes on one side, with fields to the right, so a long window was placed facing south, inset in the wall, to form a balcony one third of the way round the Mill. The granary was already joined to the cottage, so no structural alteration was needed there, except to insert windows and a fireplace. Ben loved to have open fires, so a fireplace for wood-burning was built in the studio, but Arthur Welford was in advance of his time in thinking central heating also essential as the Mill, cottage and granary all had outside walls. He and Ben worked closely together over the planning. It was fun to watch the place taking shape.

Lennox Berkeley was also wanting somewhere in the country to work, so Benjamin asked him if he would like to share the Mill with him. Lennox would pay rent, and the granary was made into a studio for him.

In April 1938 Ben moved into his new home. There was only one serious snag, the insects which dropped on him while he was composing in the studio. The Mill had been full of grain and flour for a very long time, so the walls and woodwork had harboured creatures of all kinds and it could not be expected that they would disappear immediately. I can remember him sitting at his table with a ruler by his side and as the various creatures dropped he swatted them with the ruler. Ben did not have enough furniture to fill the place. Lennox furnished his part and as it did not seem likely that I would have a settled home for some time, I was happy for Ben to have the use of my furniture from the Frinton home which had been stored at Peasenhall.

Kit Welford and I were married at Peasenhall on January 22nd 1938. My mother-in-law was anxious to have the reception at the Hall as she had no daughters of her own, on the understanding that my sister Barbara should be the hostess in place of my mother. The question now was, who should give me away at the church? I wanted Benjamin, as he and I had been so much together. My elder brother Robert said he should, and there was practically a fight outside the Yoxford Arms where all the Britten contingent stayed the night before the wedding. My mother-in-law said I could not stay in the same house as my husband-to-be that night, as it was supposed to be unlucky. I was determined that I wanted Ben to give me away as he had looked after me when I was ill and supported me through all the dreadful years when he and I had lost both our parents, as I had tried to help him, and he did give me away.

After this, the Old Mill, Snape, as it was henceforth to be called, became not only Ben's home, but Kit's and mine as well. I was not happy staying with my in-laws, so Ben suggested that we should go to the Mill whenever we could get away from London. My husband was still a medical student at St Thomas' Hospital and not due to take his finals until later that summer.

Benjamin and Lennox worked happily together at the Mill all through that summer and the winter following. When not working, they walked or took the car to Aldeburgh to swim, or went to Peasenhall to play tennis with the Welfords. Aaron Copland, the American composer, came in the summer to stay with Ben, who had just completed his *Piano Concerto*. Wystan Auden was also a frequent visitor to the Mill until he went to fight in the Spanish Civil War, and of course Peter Pears often came as well.

Europe was in a state of unrest at that time and many of Ben's friends went to fight for freedom in Spain. Benjamin was no fighter and would have been useless with a gun, so he stayed at home and wrote music for freedom and peace. In 1937 he wrote a *Pacifist March,* to words by Ronald Duncan, for the Peace Pledge Union, which had been founded in 1934 by the Reverend Canon Dick Sheppard. In 1938 he wrote the incidental music for *Advance Democracy,* a documentary film directed by Ralph Bond in association with Basil Wright. After this, a part song for unaccompanied mixed chorus was published; to words by Randall Swingler it had the same title as the film *(Advance Democracy)* but the music was different. This was followed by *The Ballad of Heroes.*

The *Piano Concerto* was first performed at a Promenade Concert in the Queen's Hall on the 18th of August 1938, with Ben as soloist. We all went to hear the performance. During one energetic passage, one of his front studs (which he had borrowed from Kit because they were smarter than anything he had and he wanted to look his best for this important occasion) flew off and was never found again. There was quite a crowd outside the artists' entrance waiting for the pianist-composer to come out. It was the first time Benjamin had had so many admirers and so many requests for his autograph, and he was quite overcome.

Although Benjamin did not go to fight in Spain, he wanted to do something to help the anti-Fascist cause, so he agreed to give a home to a refugee child. A friend of his, Poppy Vulliamy, who was in touch with the refugee organisations in Spain, organised this for him. I offered to help Ben with any child he was sent so far as I could. The first Spanish child was a boy of about twelve. At first all went well. He could not speak English and none of us spoke Spanish, but we managed with sign language. Ben expected too much of this child and gave him various jobs to do about the place as he had to be occupied while Ben was working, but like most young of that age he was lazy, he lost the key of the woodshed and did not cooperate at all. Poor child, he was probably very unhappy! It was really a hopeless idea for Ben to have a child to look after on his own and it was decided to ask Poppy Vulliamy to find a family who could take him. I took the boy to London and saw him off to a more settled home. By that time most of the rescued children were able to return to Spain. The Civil War was over, Franco was Dictator and the country had settled down again to a peace of sorts.

Ben tried once more to help a child. This particular boy was from the east end of London. We took him to Cornwall with us, but the first night

Ben was horrified when the boy put his pyjamas over his under clothes. He didn't realize that most poor people then probably didn't have pyjamas anyway.

In serious mood. (Photo: Enid Slater. Wife of Montagu, librettist of *Peter Grimes*.)

A dedicated photograph.

Benjamin, Sophie Wyss and Humphrey.

Ben in 1938. (Photo: Enid Slater.)

Beth, engagement picture, 1937.

Ben and Beth arriving at Peasenhall Church, 1938 – he gave her away. "Ben is holding a fur, not an animal – it was January and cold."

April 1938, the Old Mill at Snape nearing completion.

Peter Pears and Ben at the Old Mill,
Snape, 1939.

Peter Pears and Joan Cross in *Peter Grimes*.

Ben, taken in America probably 1940–41, He had a chamber group there.

Glyndebourne 1947, break in rehearsal for 'Albert Herring'. (Photo: Edwin Mandenian).

15

Letters from America

Although Ben was fairly content in his life with Lennox Berkeley in Snape, he felt frustrated, and unable to make headway as a composer in this country. Many creative artists were also feeling the spread of Nazism and Fascism in Europe and the persecution of artists under those regimes. Many had already left for the new world, among them Wystan Auden and Christopher Isherwood, and Ben was very much influenced by these older men. Peter Pears was then a member of the BBC singers, and he had already been twice to the States.

It was strange that, although Ben was such a marvellous pianist he only wrote one major work for the piano, his chief creative power was writing for the voice, and there was something about Peter's voice which gave Ben what he needed. A close friend of Ben's who had known my mother well and heard her voice, remarked to me recently, that Peter's voice was very like my mother's, and she had just died. They had already become good friends in the short time they had known each other and Peter, a marvellous musician and a good scholar, was looking for something other than being a singer in a choir, so they decided to go together to make a new life in the United States.

Ben always had to have a place to live in London, and Peter had given up the flat that he was then living in, so they had found a flat in Hallam Street; where they gave a party just before they left. It was a very sad parting for me, I did not know when I would see Ben again, we had been so close, especially during the recent years. He promised to write constantly and tell us how they were managing, fortunately he was a very good letter writer, and as can be seen during the next chapters, he kept his promise. Some of the letters during the battle of the Atlantic must have been lost.

Cunard White Star "Ausonia"

May 9th 1939

My darling old Beth,
    I hope things are going well with you. I'm thinking lots of you &

Sebastian [My son Sebastian was a baby of six weeks when Ben left], & cursing myself for a fool that I have come away! However the journey so far has not been too bad, in fact in places quite exciting. To start from the beginning: The Bridges motored to Southampton to see us off – it was frightfully nice of them. And we got your wire on board which was very nice – thanks alot for it. And then started I suppose very much the same kind of life that you had going to Jamaica [our honeymoon]. I hoped to do lots of work & reading – but somehow one never had the energy to do it – the perpetual eating & deck tennis, ping-pong & shuffle bottom etc. take up too much time, & energy.

We had two days of severe gales, & the ship jumped & bumped terrifyingly, but neither of us were sick & only exhausted at having to adjust ourselves to the angle of the ship. Then a wonderful day of icebergs, not very large, but we had to stop altogether for about 16 hours & the bergs banged against the side – a marvellous sight tho'. Then fog – that was beastly – and again we had to stop for about 12 hours, while the siren blew & blew. Then much more ice yesterday (Sunday), at the entrance of the St. Lawrence – & a few Aurora Boreales. So we've seen abit of life! although we're nearly three days late in doing so.

Passengers are very dull: There is a Mr. Yateman who wrote ½ of 1066 & all that, who is amusing in a rather professional way. A Sir something Drummond who knows all about Zululand. Two boys sons of Missionaries – who are wild beyond imagination – reaction to the Puritanical parents I suppose.

Plans: so far expect to stay three days or so in Montreal – then Ottawa or Toronto & then we've heard of a nice shack place up on the Hills near there, & expect to stay there for about a month or so. Then across to Vancouver. I'll let you know more later – meanwhile please keep on writing to Toronto. Hope you went to Snape after all & enjoyed the car!

My love to all the large Family. Has Kit gone into Hospital yet? Don't forget please use Snape as much as possible.

Much love, my dear.
Benjamin.

We did go to Snape as often as we could, but Kit was doing his job at St Thomas' Hospital, which he was fortunate enough to be given after he had qualified, so we could not go as often as we would have liked. Also Lennox was still there and, although we kept to Ben's part of the house and Lennox was very nice about our being there, he was paying rent and we did not want to encroach on him too much.

Gray Rocks Inn
St Jovite Station
Province of Quebec
Canada

June 5th 1939

My dear old Beth,

Thanks alot for your nice long letter. I was frightfully pleased to get it. I couldn't imagine why I hadn't heard from you – since I thought you would have had my letters long since. Anyhow I had a letter from Wulff this morning by Air Mail – so there's no excuse for letters taking a long time now, although it's much more expensive. Don't write by it unless it is very important!

So far the trip's being a great success. We are getting on well together & no fights. This place is just heavenly & it is sickening we've got to leave it on Wednesday. The people are very nice – we have become bosom friends of an American secretary & the daughter of the pioneer up in these parts – very nice people who take us about in cars & play tennis & golf with us lots. In fact with all those occupations & walking alot, to say nothing of work which goes pouring out – I've nearly finished a Violin Concerto since I got here – besides a job for the BBC! – time has gone very fast indeed!

You wouldn't believe how wild this part of the world is – practically no roads, & what there are are bad beyond description. Mount Tremblante which we look at is the most northerly bit of civilisation before you get to Hudson Bay nearly 400 miles – & most of it is only roughly sketched out on the map – no one's ever been there! Incredibly beautiful too.

We go to Toronto on Wednesday evening – I've got to go & see the Boosey and Hawkes people there & then Peter and I go to Grand Rapids (USA) for about a week – & then I've got to return to Toronto to have a personal interview on the radio! Before the Variations are played! 7.30 on 18th in the evening – but don't try & get it as I believe it is about 12.30 by your time! It seems odd that you are five hours in front of us all the time.

After that is not settled yet – Ottawa probably – & New York & South after that. The Vancouver car trip fell through because of the broadcast & King & Queen not being out of the way before end of June (we want to see the Tweedsmuirs who are occupied with their Gracious Majesties!) – & it takes so long to go by car – at least a fort-night.

One thing that has been a curse up here is the Mosquitoes! You'd never dream of anything so numerous – all the houses have screens on, but outside as soon as you are still for a moment on they jump – & "suck-suck" – with the result "scratch-scratch"! They're so bad that we both feel quite ill with them.

Now for your news. This is exciting about Sebastian & the musical box. But don't let him be a musician – it's too much like hard work – but I daresay you won't have entered him for King's College choir be-fore I get back.

I was <u>very</u> angry to hear that Mrs Hearn was snooty with you – she knew perfectly well that you were coming. I told her ages ago & re-peatedly. You give her socks if she's like that again! and please go alot. July will be freer I should think.

No, I wasn't <u>frightened</u> exactly on the ship – tho' I did hope that they'd got good & careful watches during the nights – & I half felt I'd go & offer myself for the job. The storm was beastly because everything bumped and creaked so – & one got so tired with the ef-fort of keeping up. But I didn't ever begin to wonder whether I felt sick!

Please give my love to Barbara will you, & tell her all the news. I will write in a few days when I get to Toronto – or anyhow Grand Rapids. I hope she's feeling better now. Where did you go for Whitsun? None of you to Snape? – or was Lennox there?

We are going for a picnic to-day – along Devil's River – that sounds romantic doesn't it? Especially as both our companions are of the fair sex & pretty fair at that! Don't be surprised if I've changed my state when I get back.

Much love, my dear old thing. I miss you lots & I wish to goodness you were here. But I'll have a look round & see whether I can find a nice practice for Kit! You'd love the country & the people arn't too bad.

My love to the family & I hope Sebastian's given up waking up in the night!

See you soon, I expect!
Love, B
Peter sends his love

PS Could you possibly ring up the flat & find out what's happened to Jackie – we haven't heard a word from him or even had any letters forwarded. If he can't remember what to do with our letters – he'd better send the whole lot to Snape – including Peter's. Please!

June 25th 1939
c/o Boosey & Hawkes
Toronto
Moskoka

My darling old thing,

I'm writing this in the train from Bala – up the Moskoka lakes to Toronto, at 11.0 pm. on Sunday. I've written a newsy letter to Barbara & I was going to send you a postcard as I wrote to you last, but I thought I would scribble a note (*if* you can read it!) saying that I thought lots about you on 17th – & how did Sebastian behave? Did he cry? I wish I'd been there to do my duty officially. [This must have been Sebastian's christening.]

Things are going quite well – though personally I'm pretty tired. They keep us so hard at it – and I've being fêted rather too much – I'm not used to that sort of thing! It even got into the papers that I went on a scenic railway!

We are going to New York on Tuesday & it looks as if it may be the same way. But we are looking for a quiet cheap place for two months – & that'll be nice. I don't know yet about the Autumn. It looks as if I shall stay over here – unless there's a war. I might as well confess it now that I am seriously considering staying over here permanently. I haven't decided of course and I'm terribly torn, but I admit that if a definite offer turned up (and there are several in the air) I might take it. Use your judgement as to whether you tell anyone – as it is so much in the air I suggest you don't.

Canada is an extraordinary place. I am <u>certain</u> that N. America is the place of the future. I wish to goodness you would come across. Would Kit necessarily want to <u>buy</u> a practice or would he work up one? But seriously – do think about it, & if I see anything at all possible I'll let you know. We've met some charming people over here – & though certainly one is worried by a lack of culture, there is terrific energy & vitality in the place.

We're just arriving in Toronto so I must stop. It strikes me that you won't after all be able to read a word of this – but perhaps it doesn't matter! All my love to all of you.

Ben.

Peter sends <u>love</u> to you all.
Please write <u>often & lots</u> – I live on letters.

A letter to Barbara, dated June 25th, 1939, sent from Bala.

Dear old Barbara,

It seems ages since I wrote to you – but really there is no time for writing nowadays. Since we left Gray Rocks on 8th we have been kept wildly at it – spend most of the time in Toronto where we were treated like royalty – someone to take the place of the king & queen I suppose! But you see in Canada & the States, people take music seriously. They've made a great fuss of us – I've had interviews with every paper (& usually center page too!) – & lunches & parties galore. Had to make speeches too! – but anyhow, here, people listen to your accent & don't bother about what you say! I'll send you some of the cuttings if I can find them – bet you'll laugh lots.

We spent five days down at Grand Rapids in the States – friends of Peter's & very nice too – then back to Toronto where we gave a duet broadcast of all my stuff – I had an interview too on the Radio before a good show of the <u>Variations</u>. They've also commissioned me to write a special piece & play it with Orchestra on August 27th – nice of them?!! Now we are spending two heavenly days up in the Moskoka Lakes a singing teacher Peter wanted to see lives up here by the side of the Lake – a grand spot. We go back to Toronto tonight & then on to <u>New York</u> on Tuesday. I'm looking forward lots to that – it ought to be very exciting. No plans yet after that – all depends on Aaron

[Copland] (you remember him!!) who we'll see there. But I expect we'll have a good time – we have so far always managed it!

I hope you're all right, my dear. I think about you lots – more than you'd imagine! Write to me as much as possible – you can't imagine how welcome letters are! By-the-way, it is better <u>always</u> to send letters to Toronto – we move about so suddenly – I got your last one lots late. Quite a good thing is to find out when the "Queen Mary" sails & to send by that.

Have you been to Snape yet? I expect your hay-fever's on the mend now – was it a bad bout this year? Peter's had it abit.

Please tell the family all the news – I'll write <u>when</u> I get the time – but as I say it is <u>very</u> difficult.

Love to Helen. Take her to Snape. <u>So sorry</u> about the Budges. It is rotten for you. Requiem aeternam dona eis.

<u>Much love, Ben</u>

Peter sends his love

July 14th, 1939

George Washington Hotel
Twenty-third Street & Lexington Avenue
N York City NY.

My darling Beth

This is only a scribbled note (a) to thank you for your letters, which I love having, please keep up the weekly bulletin; one adores letters when one is so far away & (secrets!) one occasionally feels very home-sick for ones sisters (b) to tell you to send these letters c/o Boosey & Hawkes Belwin Inc. 43-45-47, West 23rd Street, New York City (c) to tell you that Peter & I are now settled for a month up in a place called Woodstock in the Kingston District of the Hudson River (look it up on the map) near the Catskill Mts. It's very beautiful & we've rented a studio there. Aaron C[opland] is near & we have a great time alto-gether.

I'm in N. York again for a few days as the N.Y. Philharmonic Orch. have just played my Variations [on a theme of Frank Bridge] at one of their big out-of-door Stadium concerts – & it was a great success, my dear! I had to go twice onto the platform to bow – the orchestra was very pleased & so was the audience (about 5000!). The write-ups have been marvellous – so I feel rather "started" in New York now!

You would adore this city – but be abit bewildered by it, as I am now. It is very sophisticated, but charming. It is very beautiful & the sky-scrapers are <u>incredible</u>! Everso big!

Glad to hear Sebastian is well. I'm sick to be missing so much of him as it'll be a lovely period of his development. But <u>all</u> periods'll be the best – you proud old mother, you!

I think of you lots & lots my dear – & wish you were here. No more developments about the little matter I wrote about last time – but I feel much the same. I hope Kit's back with you now. Did you enjoy Snape?

Much love to you all & to Barbara when you write.

Ben.

How's the new maid?

Woodstock, N.Y.

July 28th 1939.

My darling old Beth,

I always seem to be writing to you just as the Mail for England is departing & am consequently very rushed for time. The truth is that one is kept very occupied these days. Peter & I do all our own house-work(!) & gosh, what a time it takes – nearly as bad as W. Cottage Road! [the flat we had shared together].

Our days are generally something like this:

get up – 8.30 (with luck)
Finished getting breakfast & washing up and cleaning up – 10.30
Then work (got lots to do too – especially with this commission for Toronto on top of everything) with an interval for cold scrappy lunch until – say – 4.30.

Then we walk along to Aaron's cottage, where we bathe in stream & sun till – 6.0.

Then tennis perhaps till 7.30 or 8.0 Then the big meal of the day at a snack bar called Trolley Car; & after that either here or at Aaron's we gossip or play piano or go to the cinema at Kingston 9 miles away. So we're occupied – you see!

Of course this drought has been awful – everyone is running out of water – & gosh, the heat! I can't imagine the Tropics much hotter! Actually the weather has broken now – & tho' it is still very hot, it has been raining for 2 days solidly.

No plans yet for future – immediate ones are – we're here till 20th Aug – then New York to see Peter off on 23rd by Queen Mary – then I go up to Toronto to play new piece on the Radio; I shall probably go up to Bala again for a few days: what I shall do in September isn't settled yet, but I may go to New Mexico to see Wystan. Anyhow I shan't be in New York till October I don't think. Then we'll see how things turn out.

Let me know all the news. I suppose Kit's at Beckenham now? Are you with Elinor – it is so difficult to keep track of dates – being so far away. I hope you're happy with Sebastian – obviously he's the best baby yet – everyone says so to me anyhow!

Much love – please give Barbara my love & all the news – I'll write by next Boat.

Greetings to all 3,   Benjamin.

Look out for bombs, please!

16

Outbreak of War

When the second world war was declared on September 3rd 1939, Kit, Sebastian and I were at Peasenhall staying with the Welford parents. I shall never forget the feeling of absolute horror and despair that overcame us all. We all remembered the last war, Kit and I as children very vaguely, but Arthur Welford had fought in Greece, and become prematurely bald and unwell as a result of these years.

September '39

U.S.A.

My darling Beth,

I am enclosing this in an air-mail to Barbara & I hope it eventually gets to you. So it has happened. I am thinking of you literally the whole time and wishing I were with you, if it would do any good. I am hoping that by some means or other you & Sebastian will have moved to Peasenhall & that Kit will be with you. His locum must be nearly over now.

Barbara will tell you what little news there is. One is keeping sane, in the middle of these screaming headlines & blaring hysterical radios, by working hard, & playing music, reading, & generally dosing oneself with art. It is the only thing that gives one any faith in mankind at these times. We are staying with some friends of Peters [the Mayers] who are as nice & sensible as possible & an infinite comfort. How I wish you were here too. Sebastian must be heavenly now – lovely that he doesn't know what's happening. I wish you would send some photos sometime – he must be getting large. Does he still laugh as much as ever?

I went to Toronto the other day to play on the Radio a new piece I've just written with orchestra. It went well – but I wasn't feeling so happy about things that I could enjoy it as much as normally. I flew there & back – & enjoyed that; first time since that little episode over the North Sea in January! Please give my love to the family W. and tell D [Dorothy, my mother-in-law] I'll write as soon as I have time but I'm pretty occupied at the moment. I enjoyed her last letter lots. America is nice – & I have grand plans for the future & intimately connected with you – too!

Much love and be sensible and not self-sacrificing ever!

Love to Kit and my Godchild
Ben.

Kit was free then, finished his hospital job, and had been doing a Locum, thinking what to do next. It was the most wonderful weather and we drove most days to Minsmere on the coast, taking the baby with us. Driving through the country lanes, it was so peaceful and beautiful. Had the world gone mad? Could we really be at war again? The horror of war was swiftly brought home to us sitting on the beach at Minsmere. A large cargo boat passing out to sea, nothing else in sight. Suddenly her bows shot into the air, and it seemed only moments before the boat gave a great heave and disappeared. What could we do? We were miles from a telephone, there was no one in sight. We could only hope the Coastguards had seen it as well. We heard nothing. Everything was secret in those days. The boat must have hit a mine.

Long Island Home,
Amityville, N.Y.

October 19, 1939

My darlingest Beth,

I was sick when I read in your letter that you hadn't had any communications for so long from me. I hope that by now that you will have got my letters. Please don't think that I've forgotten you! Why I don't write every day is because Air-mail is so beastly expensive – & it is the only mail that gets to places in reasonable time. Your letter took just three weeks! You seem horribly far off with communications so bad. I try to write to you & Barbara every week alternatively – & please tell the other one all the news – that sort of thing.

Actually one is terribly busy here. You see it is not like England where ones name is known musically – here people are willing to be impressed, but one has to work hard to keep it up. And at the moment one is in the between stage of – "well, if you produce the work we'll do it" – & one has to sit down & do it! However things might be much worse. The only part that is so awful, is that I find working so difficult. Thinking of you all day & wondering what is happening now. The papers are hysterical here you complain that you're not told enough – well, we're told too much. And half of it is false rumours. I nearly died when I heard that the length of the East Coast had been raided, but then it turned out that it was only a scare. . . .

The Mayers continue to be as sweet as possible. The fact that they are Europeans is so comforting at this time. Americans are awfully inclined to treat the whole thing as an awfully interesting stage play, & applaud or hiss as they feel inclined. There is no doubt on whose side their sympathy lies. Something like ½% sympathise with the Nazis I believe. . . .

I see lots of Wystan; it is nice to have him around. Also Aaron Copland – although he's gone off to Hollywood to do a film at the moment. Wystan & my opera is settled for Broadway when we have done it. We'll have our work cut out doing it, I feel! I've also completed the rest of the *Illuminations* for Sophie to do in November – somewhere in London I believe, but I thought concerts were stopped? Ask Ralph when because I should love you to hear them – they're my best so far. You heard the grand news about the first performance of the Violin Concerto in New York Philharmonic? So I shouldn't be too bad tempered – but if only you were over here. I think we'll have to arrange this, Beth, you come over & keep house for Peter and me! Goodness me, I wish you could persuade Kit to try that. I know it sounds hopeless, but at these moments anything is worth trying! My great idea is for all my friends (& nice relations!) to come & live over here, & if the situation's possible we could go back to England for holidays. Think it over! Barbara seems tied to Helen & her job – but it looks abit as if her job won't last very long – –??

Thank you for seeing about the Mill & furniture. Why couldn't you & Barbara live there & keep it up? I might send you money from time to time. It's very cheap, living in Snape.

Please forgive this rambling incoherent letter – but I've been dictating (!) letters all the morning and I'm very wuzzy! Beata eldest Mayer daughter, who is a trained sec, is living here at the moment, & has been helping me with my overdue correspondence!! There's, as usual, lots to do.

My love to everyone. I shall be writing to D in a day or so. How's everyone? I <u>loved</u> the photos of Sebastian & you. You both look grand. I was terribly sentimental when I got them. I think he looks lovely, especially the close up of him – & the one on your shoulder. You look grand too – o, how I'd love to see you again. But sometime we MUST. Give my love to Barbara & say how much I appreciate her long letters. She really is writing marvellous ones – & they are well known in the State of New York. I'll be writing to her next mail.

xxxxooooxxxx

Ben.

Although the Blitz on London did not start until early September 1940, throughout the war there was enemy activity, on the East Coast and near the coast. Enemy planes came over the villages gunning people in the streets. One such event happened at Peasenhall while we were staying there, when a plane flew all the way down the village street on a Sunday afternoon. Fortunately there was no one about, being at home eating Sunday lunch.

At the beginning of the war panic set in and evacuees were rushed out of London. Barbara was a health visitor then, in Hampstead, looking after six clinics, assisted entirely by voluntary workers. The powers that be decided that all pregnant women must leave London and Barbara had to escort a busload into deepest Hertfordshire. Their destination was strictly secret and Barbara had to pacify frantic husbands who wanted to know where their wives were going. She could only hope that the excitement would not bring the babies on before their time, as she was single-handed. They arrived at a Rectory, where to say the least they had a very grudging reception, but she went thankfully back to London with the bus driver, having delivered her charges without mishap. The mothers-to-be were all back in London almost as soon as she was, finding their own way home.

Long Island Home,
<u>Amityville, N.Y.</u>
(AMITYVILLE)

My darling Beth,

There really isn't any news – I told Barbara everything in my last letter – which I hope you heard about, and I do nothing here except work, while Peter goes around looking for possible jobs; – But I couldn't bear the thought of an air-mail going to England without something in it for you from me!

Life here is as good as possible under the circumstances. It is very quiet (except when the patients start kicking up a fuss & screaming & shouting the place down!) and I'm doing lots of work. Mrs. Mayer is the most marvellous person – motherly and comforting. The fact that she's European is so important at these times. She is terribly keen on music – we spend all our time at that, it seems. The children and Mr. Mayer are nice too – and so are the Titleys, in whose house we are actually staying (tho' we eat chez Mayer). We expect to stay here until we know definitely about things (money, etc.) and we <u>may</u> take a small house in Amityville – which is a lovely place and the sea looks more like the North Sea and the coast like the East Coast than can be believed. I may be having a good commission to write a big work through the British Council, but until that is signed & settled I am not rejoicing! I've had too many false alarms in my day! But I'll let you know of course as soon as anything materialises. <u>If</u> I can afford a house – I want so much to get you all over here – I'm building <u>such</u> castles in the air! Do write a note as soon as you can saying how you are. Try air-mail direct to here it's so much quicker. Other letters are held up terribly.

Airmail just going so I must stop.

Love to everyone (including Robert if & when you write – tell him I'll write soon) and to D of course I hope she's well.

My love, my darling, keep well – I'm sure we shall all survive!

Benjamin

Amityville, N.Y.

November 28th 1939
My darling Beth,

I am writing this in a New York Psychiatrist's office – Dr. Squire's (alias Mrs. Titley) in whose house Peter & I are sleeping. Peter & I are in N.Y. for the day – a typical business day – seeing odd people, having lunch with an eminent organist, tea with an arty "socialite", & going to the flat of a Columbia broadcasting official after dinner to-night. I discovered yesterday that there is a Clipper going to-morrow so I brought my pen & paper up here – actually I discover that I only brought one sheet of air-mail paper & so the letter'll have to be shorter than I intended. Well – thank you <u>very</u> much for the cable. I loved having it & it was nice of you to remember your poor little bro. – especially as no one has any good words to say for him at the moment (although for anything, he can't think what he has or hasn't done!) I had a nice birthday – the Mayers were sweet and gave me lots of presents, & cake, & candles, & party. Wystan came & with Peter, Titleys & family we had a grand time. But one did miss the old family ties – gosh, it's awful how home-sick one feels – & especially Suffolk-sick – but I'm glad, overjoyed that you & Kit are at the Mill – you got my wire? . . . <u>If</u> you are having bother in keeping up the place do let me know & I'll struggle to send some more money. By-the-way, re this £50 – don't fight over it – just divide it as you both honestly think most fair – at this distance you can't tell who needs it most – & I had to send it to Barbara since it'll be most convenient for her to change the draught. So <u>don't</u> write abusing letters saying I favour one or the other – because honestly, my darling, I can't stand any more of these letters (at 3,000 distance & a war on, letters cool off & lose their points, if they're only <u>d</u>estructive criticism). Anyhow, I do want, if physically possible, you to go on living at the Mill – to regard it as <u>yours</u>, not to think of letting it (unless of course you can't possibly keep it up), & from time to time I'll send you what monies I can spare. I was <u>terribly</u> pleased with your last letter – it was so nice & chatty, telling me all the things I wanted to hear – I adore hearing about Sebastian, he sounds a grand kid. If I saw him now, I bet I wouldn't recognise him!

Time's getting on & I've got this lunch date, so I must buck up. Don't worry about me old thing – I'll get along all right. People are terrifically kind & I'll never be destitute or starve! It is horrible, of course, & we get an overdose of radio, & paper news – & one feels hopeless and distraught – poor old Kit, I bet he feels like hell. But tell him to read lots (Jane Austen!) and play the gramophone (Mahler!).

I'm working hard – just starting a new opera with Wystan – but I find working terribly difficult.

Much much love to you all three. <u>Remember</u>, stay at the Mill, consider yourselves joint owners of it, & I'll help out with ex. if poss.

xxxxooo   Ben   xxxooo   Love from Peter

Barbara's job came to an end because the clinic where she worked was a voluntary one and a lot of children left London to go to the country or were sent to the U.S.A. It was not long, however, before she was appointed Assistant Superintendent of the Child Welfare Department of the Middlesex Hospital in London. She was happy there, for they were connected with the big teaching hospital and had the medical students to instruct about baby care, although she told us that on the whole they were bad mannered and could not care less about babies. But the pediatricians came to the clinics so there was plenty of life and interest.

Dec. 14th 1939

Long Island Home
Amityville, N.Y.

My darling Beth,

The Clipper goes on Saturday & so I want to get a note to you to wish you a happy Xmas – as far as is possible. Anyhow – forget the bloody business for the Festive Season – only live in the immediate present (unless you're being bombed) & try & enjoy yourself if you can. I'm hoping to have a letter from you saying that you're all going to be at the Mill. That would be a heavenly thought for me – even if I can't be there myself it's the next best thing for the nearest & dearest to be there! I've made an effort to get some small presents to you – but don't be disappointed if nothing turns up. We shall all be here – they're a nice family & we shall have a jolly time – at least an effort at it, since every member has a load of things on his (or her) mind to prevent him (or her) being carefree. I should adore you to meet the family – they are quite your cup of tea. There are endless worries here – which I'll tell you about when we meet. I've written lengthily to Lennox about you and the Mill – so that should all be cleared now. The Flat seems settled too – so the immediate worries are over. But *don't* leave the Mill unless imperative – it's lovely to know you're there. Much love to you and Sebastian – and his teeth – he sounds fine!

Love,   B.

Dec. 14, 1939

c/o Mrs. W. Mayer
Long Island Home,
Amityville, N.Y

My dearest Kit,

I was highly delighted with your letter – it was the wisest, & most

124

informative, & consequently hopeful letter that I have received from England yet. When I have more time I will answer it in detail & give a similar picture of U.S.A. But at the moment I have only time for a scribbled "best wishes" letter (a forlorn hope, I realise), but after my present rush of work I'll write properly. Anyhow I am from time to time posting you copies of the New Yorker, because in my opinion that is the best picture of the States you can get. It has the failures as well as the virtues – & both are many. I am at the moment making enquiries about medical conditions over here – entrance bothers & quotas & I hope to be able to write fully about this soon. It is the best thing I'm convinced. Your letter wasn't censored – as far as I could see wasn't even opened. I dare say the New Yorker will be. You might tell me if my letters are. I find it difficult to get letters to the Scherchens in Cambridge (German émigrés). Best wishes, old thing; have a good time – stay as long at the Mill as you can – I like to have you there.

Yours ever   Benjamin

We went to the Welfords at Peasenhall for Christmas, although we would much rather have stayed on our own at the Mill. Of course it was very comfortable at Peasenhall, with servants and luxury in every way, and they liked to have their first grandchild with them, but Kit and I always found it a strain. There were constant rows between Kit and his father, mostly about Kit's untidy habits. Perhaps as a reaction against his mother's excessive desire to have an immaculate and beautiful home, Kit seemed to do everything to annoy her. I do not blame my mother-in-law. I suffered all the rest of my married life from Kit's lack of care of anything that I tried to make nice.

Although Ben was anxious for us to emigrate to the U.S.A. and for Kit to find some medical employment or a practice over there, we never really considered going, much as I would have dearly loved to be near him.

c/o Dr. W. Mayer,
Long Island Home
Amityville, N.Y.

New Year's Eve, 1939
My darling Beth,
    This is only a note to wish you a happy New Year – faint hope, but if possible a better one than 1940 [sic], which shouldn't be difficult.

Heaven knows when you'll get this letter, the posts seem to get worse & worse, now that the air mail's so disorganised, but you may get it in time for next New Year's day!

First of all – what sort of Christmas did you have? All at Peasenhall I expect? Hope it was not too gloomy and that all the festivities weren't entirely "blacked-out". God – it must be hellish for you! You can't imagine how much I feel for you, & think of you. When I read all these things in the papers (half of which aren't – luckily – true) it is odd to think that they're happening to <u>you</u> – the nice person I shared 559 Finchley Road with – that <u>your</u> food's being rationed, that <u>your</u> M.G.'s headlights are dimmed etc. etc. I'm feeling abit blue tonight – God how I hate anniversaries – & what with my birthday, Mum's birthday, Xmas & now New Year's Eve – we seem to have had a good supply of them recently. Anyhow – thank you ever so much for your letter. It was worth £50 to get cheerful letters from you & Barbara! But mind you, don't start writing grumpy ones again, because it won't always work!

We had a a nice Xmas – the Mayers gave us all a fine one. In the German custom it was Xmas Eve which was the great hour – at about 6 o'clock a bell was rung & in we all trouped into the living-room & there was an enormous Xmas tree hung all over with candles, candies & cookies & all round the room in little piles were our presents – & lots too – everyone was very generous to us – which made up for lack of correspondence from England! Did you, by the way, get some little presents from me – I shan't be surprised if that little scheme went wrong – but anyhow the <u>thought</u> was there!

I played Young Apollo on Columbia a week or so ago – it went well & everyone was pleased. Ralph Hawkes arrives to-morrow & I go with him to Chicago (about 1500 miles!) the day after – & play the Concerto on 15th – It is going to be nice to see him, but I don't want to leave here. I am becoming a very retiring boy at the moment – I loathe going up to New York, & all I want to do is to sit still & play Chinese checkers – that's a game that is rampant over this Continent at the moment!

Wystan's been here for a week & we've done lots of work on the opera – I know you'd like it – it's full of nice tunes & blues & things. No date for production yet.

Must stop now as all the mid-night celebrations are about to begin. Ugh! Wish you were here my dear.

Much love to my God-child – send a photo sometime. He sounds sweet. Also to Kit – tell him to write to me again soon.
                             & lots to you, yourself, darling
                                    Be careful,
                                        Ben.

Could you be a saint & forward these letters for me – air-mail is so expensive.
Laulie: Miss Austin, Flat no. 4, Gambier Terrace, Liverpool
Mr. Nicholson.

In January 1940 the doctor at Orford, a village twelve miles from Snape, became ill and Kit was asked to go. Since Christmas we had had snow and ice and Orford was cut off except by river. The road from Snape to Aldeburgh was just possible, but the river Alde from Aldeburgh to Snape was blocked by great chunks of ice. I drove Kit with difficulty along a hazardous icy snow-covered road to Aldeburgh and then along the beach road to Slaughden, where a boat was waiting to take Kit the rest of the way to Orford. It was a strange feeling to see my husband go off into the blue, not knowing when I would see him again. He waved to me until he passed the Martello Tower which stands just beyond the narrowest strip of shingle, which divides the sea at that point from the river; which then turns inland towards Orford.

The Martello Towers were built at the time when it was believed that Napoleon would invade England. A year or so before the war a wealthy lady had bought the one at Slaughden and did it up, building a kitchen on the top with glass all round, with a fantastic view of the river and the sea. She had moved in just before the war started, but was made to leave, the rumour being that she was thought to be a spy and might signal to the Germans from her tower, though she was not a spy at all. As soon as the place was abandoned the road which had been built was gone in the next big storm and the Martello Tower started to crumble again.

The Martello Tower area was one of Benjamin's favourite haunts in winter. There he could be alone between the river and the sea, with hundreds of waders on the mud flats. He was very interested and knowledgeable about all birds, but was especially fond of the sea and river birds. A friend of mine, Ruth Gathorne-Hardy, related to me the following incident. Ruth's daughter Rose was upstairs at their home in Aldeburgh, studying for an exam, in the room from which she could see the Martello Tower. Suddenly Rose came running downstairs, seized the telescope and ran upstairs again and said to Ruth: "I <u>must</u> go, there is someone standing near the Martello Tower, someone marvellous, I simply must see who it is." Her mother thought she had gone mad as Rose rushed out of the house. About half an hour later she returned. "Well," asked Ruth, "who was it?" "Ben," replied Rose. "Did you speak to him?" – they knew him well. "No," said Rose, "I put my hair over my face and ran past him."

Jan. 21st 1940

c/o Dr. W. Mayer
Long Island Home
Amityville, N.Y.

My darling old thing,

I was highly delighted with your letter (Jan. 4th [Pop's birthday] – <u>another</u> anniversary, how they get one down!), which came after what seemed a long silence. But anyhow one is letter-greedy nowadays and it probably wasn't as long as it seemed. It was a beauty – & told me lots of news about things I wanted to know. You do write nicely, you know – just anything that comes into your head, about everyday things, which is what one really is interested in. . . . . . I was overjoyed with the calendar – & it makes my heart beat faster every time I see it – it was a <u>grand</u> idea. I love the picture of the Aberdeen Trawler – & all the pictures are excellent and remind me –o, how they remind me! However –

Well – there is so much news that I don't know where to begin – all letters must necessarily (??) be so sketchy in detail; <u>when</u> we meet you'll hear all the details – shall we ever stop talking? I had a <u>terrific</u> success in Chicago – like one dreams of! 14 calls – & cheers & shouts of speech! I had a slight accident with the piano at the beginning of the Concerto – the piece of wood which keeps the keys in place became displaced – & I had to stop the orchestra & apologise to the audience (which they <u>adored</u> – my English accent!) before recommencing. That won their hearts I think. Anyhow I'm re-booked for Chicago in May. So <u>that's</u> good. I had two weeks' trip. Started in Champaign, Illinois (flew there), where I heard lots of wind-bands and met conductors – got to do an article on it for a paper – then I went to Chicago where I rehearsed the Concerto. Then to Grand

Rapids, Michigan (where I was in the summer), saw lots of people I had to (some friends, some business), flew back to Chicago – with vile cold & 'flu (temperature was 14° below 0°* one day – you've never dreamed of such cold!) which has only just cleared up. I was back in Chicago on 11th, where I had a terrific time – with interviews & parties (British Consulate threw one for me!) – & after the show on Monday flew home. Marvellous journey – we had tail-wind, & did it (to New York) in 3 hours 20 minutes (it's about 780 miles!). I felt completely dead on arrival – but I'm fine now – Mrs. Mayer is such an angel & looks after me like a mother. Besides Ralph Hawkes has been down here which is fine. It was lovely to see him – could tell us so much about general conditions. He's going to be over here for a long time I think – & is full of schemes.

Now, my dear, I am so glad you're back at Snape. I am perfectly all right as regards cash – & if you're in need of any, let me know at once. You see we're living very cheaply & altho' we're not rich, we're managing quite nicely. We've got to make new plans for the future as things won't always be as easy as they are now – but we'll let you know as soon as anything is settled. I'm writing to Barbara to tell her to use the money – to send you some for the upkeep of the Mill. I want you to consider yourselves (you & Kit) as temporary owners of the Mill – to do anything you like with it. I <u>don't</u> want you to let it – unless you want money yourself – or Nicholson wants money for me – because anyhow you <u>can't</u> send money out of the country for me, you know? <u>Do</u> try & live there indefinitely – it's the next best thing to living there myself to know that you are there.

I'm all right – I felt abit bad over Xmas – & abit hopeless about the future – but since Ralph turned up & I had the success in Chicago, I feel better. And now to get <u>you</u> over here. What plans! –

Love to Kit & Sebastian. Tell Kit to write again. I love his letters.

Please excuse writing – but I'm snowed under with important proofs to be corrected at the moment – & I wanted to catch this mail.

* The weather – not <u>my</u> temperature!!

xxxooooxxxx   Love.

Ben.   Love from Peter.

Of course we were very glad to get Ben's letter telling us to use the Old Mill and to have the feeling that we had a home to go to. We would do our best to look after the place for him in case he would come home soon and live there himself. There had been no more talk of his taking out papers to become a citizen of the U.S.A. and we hoped that was the end of that idea.

17

Dilemmas

Barbara and I were getting increasingly worried, as we had heard nothing since Ben's letter of Jan. 21st telling us that he had had flu – However at last came a letter from Peter.

Amityville

Tuesday Feb. 20th.

My dear Beth

At the moment the weather is so awful over here with gales and ice and snow that the Clippers are being put off every day longer and longer so that by the time I finish this letter and post it, Ben may have written already himself. But the reason I am writing just now is to tell you that Ben has been ill in bed but is now very nearly allright though still in bed. I'll start at the beginning – You know he went to Chicago last month to play his concerto and all, and was away 2 weeks in the bitterest weather (12° below zero, etc.) and he came back with a horrible cold and feeling lousy – well, he stayed in bed for a day or so but I think he never quite got rid of his cold, and on Thursday night (the 8th Feb.) he had a long and horrible nose bleed which left him pretty weakish – and it seems that a streptococcus of some sort seized upon that moment to attack him and of course found him pretty easy material. He got up Friday and Saturday but his face was sore, his nose blocked and a rash on his chin. He stayed in bed Sunday and has been there since. His temperature ran high – up to 104° and a bit on the Wednesday – You can guess it was a bit alarming – Luckily he was in the hands of many doctors (almost too many!) and Dr. Mayer who was in charge was confident about it, but when his temperature suddenly went up to 107° for a bit last Sunday night, he got a specialist to come down on Sunday and look him over. Well apparently he's allright and taking it very well (heart chest lungs, etc. in perfect condition) but his tonsils are quite rotten apparently and must come out at the first suitable moment (perhaps June). Also he has to take it very easy indeed for 3 or 4 weeks, as I gather after these sort of things there are always possibilities of complications (the kidneys are always the danger). So he's having an easy time and in bed for another week or so –

Friday Feb. 23rd (Sorry, the clipper was again postponed, so I put off writing more). Ben continues getting better and should be out of bed in a day or two. The specialist was emphatic that he mustn't get out of bed at all until his temperature was completely normal for four days, and as it generally goes up a few points in the evening, he's still there. Beata Mayer (the eldest daughter) who is a trained nurse, did night duty with him for a week, and now she stays with him most of the day. She was quite marvellous. But now I am back in the room with him, and he really is pretty well, except that he is rather weak still, and his face still irritates rather at night. They are being exceedingly thorough (as well as being marvellously kind) and his urine is being analysed twice a week, and from time to time they test his blood and his throat – swab. But everyone agrees that as long as he's careful and looks after himself, there's not the least likelihood of anything untoward happening – and believe me, he will be looked after very well here, you may be sure. He's very cheerful, considering the boring business of being two weeks and more in bed. Everyone adores him here, and can't do enough for him – He need never be alone unless he wants to be, and there are always people to talk or read to him, there's a portable radio by his bedside, in fact he's in clover – and really getting better every day. He's full of musical ideas, and has a little sketchbook by his bedside (à la Beethoven!) which he fills with notes. Mrs. Meyer has written a note to Barbara, I think, and don't be alarmed for a moment, Beth, because he will get all the attention he can here. We'll see to it.

How are you all? I should love to see Sebastian again – he looks fine from his pictures. Give my love to Kit and yourself and D. Look after yourselves.

Yours ever   Peter.

There's going to be a Contemporary Music Festival here in October and Ben's been asked to be on the Committee, along with Bartok etc. – very good!

At last, came a letter from Ben himself, dated March 1st.

Saturday 24th Feb. 1940

My darling Beth

Please forgive the long silence, but I gather that Peter has explained things – & I hope I won't seem so unbrotherly when you've read his letter. Anyhow its ages since I had a letter from you! I can't remember actually whether I answered the last one with photos of Sebastian in. Anyhow I adored them – he looks a grand kid – give him his godfather's love won't you. I liked his signature in Kit's letter too – shows his uncle's influence! Thank Kit too for his excellent letter. I will answer it as soon as get sufficiently "up" to hold a pen & think distinctly! I hope things are going on well with you still. Has Kit any form of job – or will he just wait until this bloody war is over? It's awfully funny – being in bed one has just got miles away from it – just like being up in the stars. It has really been a marvellous rest – & I feel fine now – only longing for the rash-irritation to go – which must be soon now. I have had really marvellous nursing! Beata is a trained nurse & managed all the bed-pans etc. marvellous – although I can't pretend I like them (B.P. I mean!) – do you remember when you had to bother with all that? Peter has been sweet & nothing too much trouble for him & everyone is marvellous. I couldn't have better attention even at Snape – so don't worry will you! there's nothing to worry about at all – I am fine & will be better than ever before.

I will write next week when I'm convalescing. I shall have lots of time then. Write soon & tell me all the news. Love to all. Hope Kit occasionally gets a New Yorker.

Much love,
Ben

March 15th 1940

Amityville

My darling Beth,

Just a scribble to inform you that I've taken my first motor-ride across to the Mayer cottage for lunch and am feeling fine. I hope you weren't scared at the absence of letters or Peter's letter – but things always seem so much worse at a distance.

How are you? Is Kit still at Orford Tell him I <u>will</u> write his letter in a day or so – but the old energy hasn't returned yet! You should have seen my beard and hair . . . it was marvellous . . . . just like Jagger Chraggers. <u>And</u> I've got all new skin over my face, hands & feet – so for once I'm quite clean! (don't whisper it about, but it's possible that I've had a strange kind of scarlet fever!!).

Much love to Kit and god child. Will write properly in a day or two.

Hope Mill's good – what about some photos of it & you

Love   Benjamin

On March 31st 1940 Peggy [Brosa] writes from the Hotel Wellington, 7th Avenue, NY:

Dear Beth

I said I would write and tell you my personal impression of Ben, so here it is! The first time we saw him down at Amityville, we got a bit of a shock; one could see he'd been really *ill*, and he was still very feeble and soon tired, also he hadn't had his hair cut for *ages,* so it was like a bush and made his face look so small and pale; however, he bucked up tremendously and he and Tony got to work on the concerto at once. The Mayers evidently adore him and wait on him hand and foot – it's lucky he isn't spoilable, as they certainly do their best! You've nothing to worry about regarding his being well looked after and happy, and now after the really terrific strain of going through those two concerts, considering everything, he stood it quite *amazingly* well. It *was* a strain too! He came up for rehearsals and stayed at Ralph Hawke's apartment – Peter also came and stayed somewhere too. Of course shoals of Mayers came for the concerts, and took them both back after the 2nd. I haven't heard anything of them since, but we hope to go down one day this week. I expect you'll have heard all about the concerts from Ben, and probably from the Mayers too. I'm afraid I was, as usual, too scared to go in front – I came back to the Hotel and said my prayers with my thumbs crossed!! But the accounts of the performances are tremendously enthusiastic, and the Press on the whole is *just* – the ones that matter are splendid, and some of the others are *frightfully* funny! I expect Ben will send you some extracts, but anyway some will appear in the Boosey-Hawkes little monthly paper "Tempo", and I expect Mr. Hawkes will have one sent to you – anyway, if you sent them a p.c. I'm sure they'd let you have one. I delivered your letter and parcel, which Ben was delighted with. Really he is much *much* better and, if he takes things quietly, he'll soon be quite strong again, so you haven't anything to worry about, and he's in splendid hands. I hope you are all well and that Sebastian is all right again.

With love   Yrs.   Peggy Brosa.

That was a marvellous letter and stopped us worrying for the time being. Peggy could never go to any of Toni's concerts because she got into a state of panic; she went away somewhere and hid until it was over.

After Kit's job at Orford was finished and the snow departed, he hung around for a while wondering what to do next. So far there was no sign of his being called up and he thought he might as well look for another locum. One of the doctors in a partnership at Swaffham in Norfolk had joined the Army and they were looking for someone to take his place. Kit applied and was taken on as a locum for as long as he could stay.

The weather was very fine that summer and we were able to be out quite a bit. One fine afternoon in June 1940, we were all having tea in the garden, there was not a cloud in the sky, when suddenly we were covered with smuts. There was a white cloth on the table, which made the smuts more noticeable. We looked up in amazement. Where could they have come from? We did not know what was happening at Dunkirk, until the news began to drift through. The smuts must have come from the battle there and from the smoke of the many boats and ships that were fetching the men away from France. It seemed hardly possible that the smuts could have drifted so far, but the wind being southerly blew them across the North Sea to Norfolk.

Next came a letter to Kit, from Ben.

April 4th 1940

Long Island Home,
Amityville, N.Y.

My dear Kit,
    I got your last long & extremely interesting letter when I was in

New York last week, & as I was feeling extremely low, being convalescent after this beastly strep, bug, it cheered me up enormously. It is so grand to hear all you're doing & with your extremely intelligent comments – besides you write about the places and people I want to hear about. When one is as far as this I find one doesn't think of England in terms of Chamberlain, or London – but in terms of Suffolk, East Anglianites, and one's friends.

Although I was sick that you've had to leave the Mill, I was glad for your sake that you got a job, & delighted that it was a country one such as you like, I know. I don't remember Swaffham well – but I have a vague idea I've had a lunch at the George. I'm hoping to hear soon that you've got a nice cottage to live in for the period you'll be there – which I hope will be long, at anyrate for the duration of this wretched squabble. Thanks for looking after the Mill so well – I'm sorry that you had the bother with the burned-out pump engine – hope it didn't cost much. If there's any outstanding account to be settled, you'd better send the bill to Nicholson (not that he's got much money to pay it with, I'm afraid, but it'll look nicer on <u>his</u> desk than <u>yours</u>!). Barbara says she'll help you to pay for Hart.

Well – we seem to have had a few excitements here. I managed, the first time for 2 months, to get into New York to hear Toni Brosa & Barbirolli's boys play my Violin Concerto last week. The bug hasn't completely left me yet – I still get periodic sore throats & a form of Uticaria on my face – but I dare say till I have the old tonsils removed I shan't get completely fit. I've had one of the best New York internists, Dr. Benjamin Ashe, looking after me – in addition to Dr. Mayer, & 3 or 4 other M.D.'s round here! – & he isn't likely to let any harm come to me – so you might reassure Beth & Barbara on that point! I don't think I'll have to face Tonsilectomy until the Fall. Anyhow I was able to make the platform in Carnegie Hall – & bow to the cheers. I had an excellent show (Toni played marvellously) & a wonderful reception. The criticisms were pretty violent – either pro. or con. The N.Y. Times old critic (who is the snarkyest & most coveted here) was won over, so that was fine. But two gave me hell in such personal terms that opinion is that they were political. One of them compared me to the Bermuda crisis (seizing of American mail-) & said it was risky, at this moment of shakiness in the British foreign policy, to produce such a work?!! and said I was an international incident. I will try & get copies of some of these & send them to you, because they're very funny –

especially one which called me a "kick-in-the-pants" of a young Englishman – I was also called "gangling" – "loose-jointed" . . . . . . these Americans! However it's all publicity.

I want to give you a rough idea of how this country strikes one, because I hope one day that you'll consider making it at least your temporary home, but it is an almost impossible job – because it simply isn't a <u>country</u>. What one state thinks will be laughed at by 45 of the others – what is possible for the West is impossible for the East – the New Yorker is as much like the Southerner as a Norwegian is like a Turk – and says so too. There is only one thing in common with them at the moment & that is disagreeable – that is that they are all <u>American</u> – & chauvanistically so, I'm afraid. They're fed up with Europe – they didn't like it's peace – and they're suspicious of it's war. They're full of advice as how to run the rest of the world – & refuse to take any of the consequences. (I will paint the <u>blackest</u> side of America, first!). Their politics are the dirtiest so far (except perhaps Canada, which has the corruption but none of the vitality of the U.S.A.) – & anything from a kidnapping case to a War will be used to their own political ends – At the moment the anti-Rooseveltians, who are anyone from the bankers to the small capitalist class, are using the German discoveries in the Polish archives (about Kennedy & Bullitt getting the States involved in war) to try & prevent Roosevelt from running a third term. In some ways this country seems to have the corruption of the Old World & little of its tradition or charm. There is, too something very frightening about this conglomeration of people (& this is true of everywhere – from East to West, & South to Middle-West) – & that is how terribly easy it is to rouse the masses (& that is nearly <u>everyone</u>) into a hysteria. The things that were done to pacifists or pro-Germans in the last war were unbelievable – & since then there have been plenty of examples of crowd-hysteria – the Klu-Klux-Klan – negro-lynchings & burnings – the Martian visit (the broadcast a year or so back), the present Dies committee with its "pro-American" searchings – in which anyone vaguely liberal is labelled as Communist & treated as such. And another dreadful shock has been the present Bertrand Russell case – in which the Irish Catholics have prevented him taking a job at the N.Y. University which was O.Ked by the board of Directors of the University & one of the student's mothers objected to a book he'd read! The Irish-Catholics are the great curse of this State – that's why the police in New York are so unscrupulous, hard & rude. The British Bobby is an angel in comparison! You see, Kit, in so many ways this country is such a terrible disappointment. Sometimes it seems to have, forinstance, all the infuriating qualities of youth without any of its redeeming qualities. Of course I judge mostly from this State – & the little of New England that I've seen – The Middle-West when I went there was quite different, & had nothing of the ultra-sophistication of, say, New York. I hate New York – Wystan compares it to a great Hotel & it's a damn good comparison. It is like the Strand Palace – all glitter, & little gold – nothing stable – everyone on the move – & terribly fashionable (in the worst sense of the word). Everything here is crazes – crazes – crazes. You see – I'm gradually realising that I'm English – & as a composer I suppose I feel I want more definite roots than other people. But against all this one must put the facts that U.S.A. is not engaged solely with killing people (altho' she may be thinking of it more every day) – enterprise still is rewarded in this country, – I'm sure there is a future for this country altho' the next decade or so may be very black. What I want so much is for you to come out here for a visit before you decide anything. I'm going to try & find out for you the medical possibilities here. You know that every emigré has to pass an exam.? Luckily speaking English, you won't have to take the language exam, which is one of the worse bogies. I have an idea that there are some states which have no exam. – I'll find that out for you. We could easily find affidavits for you – & by that time I may have taken out my 1st citizen papers – which, incidentally, aren't binding in the least. Don't take this tirade too seriously, Kit, because I'm still feeling abit (convalescentally) down after my bug – & I happen to have met lots of Americans recently (R. Hawkes gave a party for me & Toni last week) & I always feel blue after hearing Americans talk about Europe – as they all do, because, they are jealous of it – tho' God knows why at this particular moment of history!

My plans for the Summer are this: In May, I go to Chicago for a concert or two: then Peter & I settle down in a small cottage near here & work hard for the rest of the season – he to go back & forwards to N.Y. where he has lessons with Teresa (wife of Arthur) Schnabel – & me to write score after score – because altho' one might have one success, one's got to keep oneself before the public all the time. You I suppose will stay around Swaffham unless any bloody emergency calls you elsewhere (pray God it won't).

Please tell Beth that Mrs. Mayer was delighted with her letter – & that I'm in completely angelic hands here, – the Mayers, Titleys, & Peter all treat me as if I were soluble material about to take a bathe! I'll write to her by the next mail. Give my love to Sebastian – & –oh, Lord, I've forgotten his birthday – please give him the season's greetings from his devoted God-father & when I have some spare cash I'll send him some to buy a prayer-book – or what he will –

Much love, & best wishes to you all,
Benjamin.

Could you please forward the enclosed to Barbara, please? By-the-way, would you like the Mill as a present?

Ask Nicholson, if you would
. . . .!!

April 28th 1940

c/o Dr. Mayer
Long Island Home
Amityville, N.Y.

My darling old Beth,

I feel dreadful about not having written to you for so long – in fact I haven't written to anyone these last three weeks. It is partly that I simply have had no time & partly that at these beastly "eventful" times one just doesn't want to sit down & write about current events, & the trouble is one cannot think of much else to write about. Besides when posts are so slow & irregular one knows one's letters are hopelessly out of date & untopical when they reach their destination. Anyhow I am going to send this "surface" mail since the air-mail is hopeless – the Clippers have been delayed at Horta these last three weeks.

Thank you very much indeed for the socks & tie that Peggy brought with her – I am afraid I forgot to thank you in Kit's letter, but anyhow I do it now & I did really appreciate them <u>very</u> much. The socks are fine – you can't get nice woollen socks in this country, people don't seem to wear them, & the weather has been bitterly cold

– until today, which is marvellously hot & sunny, in fact I am writing this in the garden of the Mayers & nearly frizzling in the heat. The tie is just the right colour – what impeccable taste you have, old thing! Thank you also for the sweet thought. It was lovely to have Peggy arriving with a parcel from you – a real contact. She tells me she's written to you & told you all the news – probably more than I could or would think of telling you – & Mrs. Mayer's going to write again. She would have written before but has been away & busy since she got back. I'm feeling fine now. I am having a long "doing" at the dentist at the moment, & I find that the American dental art, so boosted, is not so hot after all – nothing compared with Pop or Mrs. Harwood [our dentist in London] even, but perhaps this is just the local man's failing. Certainly they have all the gadgets imaginable – including portable X-ray – but the handling is so uncouth. Then within the next month or so Peter & I are going to have our tonsils removed – & then we'll be as good as new I hope. Poor Peter, by the way, has had the most horrible carbuncle these last weeks; they are horribly painful (or rather, irritating) things. Take ages to drain. I think it's probably just one's mental condition that gets one down these days. One just feels so hopeless & helpless – & impossible to settle-down. In the normal way it wouldn't be so difficult to decide whether to stay British or change to American – but at the moment I am just marking time until I can get back to England! I suppose there wouldn't be much sense in coming at the moment – because my work is the most important thing, & I suppose it is best to stay where [one] can work most easily, & that is over here. But the idea of spending one's life here appalls me at the moment. Probably in normal times it would be O.K. – but at the present time one is inclined to see all America's bad points & England's good ones. When Americans start telling one what to do about Nazis & there are Englishmen dying by the 100 in Norway one's inclined to be unreasonable, I find.

However for the moment I am stuck here. The proposed Japanese Government commission has materialised & I now find myself faced with the proposition of writing a Symphony in about 3 weeks! Something went wrong with negotiations – which started last October & I only heard officially on Friday! However financially it relieves one of worry for abit & I should have written the work anyhow – it is a Sinfonia da Requiem, combining my ideas on war & a memorial for Mum and Pop. So I shall be pretty occupied for abit. Then I go to Chicago to do the first American show of Les Illuminations with Peter, & that'll take a week or so. Then tonsils. Then probably Mexico for quote. Then I've lots of work to do for Ralph Hawkes for the Summer – & Paul Bunyan which was held up through my being sick. God grant that something will have materialised in the world Situation by then – & that I can come home & see you!

I am longing to hear your news – I pray that you haven't had your lives affected by this new turn of events, & that you are still at Swaffham. I had a long letter from Robert all about his new school – job. I must say that I'm relieved that he is out of the way safely – surely he can't be called upon for service – with this job & his bad sight. I must write to Barbara – but anyhow give her all the news & lots of love. I hope to be able to send some more money soon to her & you all. You must let me do this as it pleases me so much! Any news of the Mill? I'm waiting for a note from Nicholson saying whether you've let it – but personally I should like to have it kept open in case Barbara &/or you want to go there ever – & I'll send money for Hart. What about Lennox sending money occasionally, because after all we're storing his furniture for him?!

Blast! – I've started a new page & I meant to stop now because it's getting so late, & I've got to go to the dentist at 9.0 in the morning. Well, I'll keep this and write some more to-morrow – I don't think it'll matter as there are probably only very few boats going at the moment, & they never advertise sailing times anyhow. So sleep well, my dear, although by now you must be well asleep – 11. p.m. here – 4 a.m. with you – you Kit & <u>Sebastian</u> – how nice it seems!!

I am sorry not to have finished this yesterday but I had a hectic day with much writing & an awful visit to the dentist – no more of that man for me – he's an old butcher, the most callous thing you could imagine. So I'll find another one in New York. I enclose a copy of the N.Y. edition of "Tempo" which reprints an article that I wrote (with Peter's considerable aid!) for the Times, & also some criticisms of the *Violin Concerto* – only the good ones of course! If I can find any other amusing things I'll put them in. This is only to bring your "lost" brother a little closer to mind! I hope it doesn't need it, because you are terribly much in my mind. Strictly entre nous, this spring gets me down alot – and homesickness is not a pleasant disease – personally I think streptococcic infection is preferable!

Much love to you all three, & good luck to you
Love   Benjamin

I had written to Elizabeth Mayer to thank her for looking after my brother so well and she replied to me on June 2nd 1940:

Amityville, N.Y.

Dear Beth

It was sweet of you to write me such a kind letter after Ben's illness, and to express your gratitude and confidence in me. I think we are the persons who should be, and are, grateful for having Ben here who is such a delightful person and a genius. He gives us so much pleasure and helps us to pass the days and weeks which are sometimes hanging heavily on our minds and hearts, with the blessing of his music. Your letter arrived on the morning of the first performance of the Violin Concerto, a wonderful experience. We have seen the Brosas very often, and I am glad for Ben as well as for us that they came out yesterday to stay in Amityville for some weeks. The city is very hot, and we are near the beach; Peggy can do her painting and Toni and Ben are playing heavenly duos. It will help Ben a lot to have friends here; he is often homesick and very worried about you all. He has told me much about his sisters and his friends, so that I seem to know you a little bit. How much I wish to know you personally as soon as possible – you may imagine. I wish particularly that I could have Sebastian here for the summer months; please, have always in your mind that a place called Amityville exists somewhere in the world, peaceful till now but who knows how long. We all think of you and the appalling times, and I wish I could help, tell me always please if I might help . . . . .

It is so hard to write letters now to friends in distress, and yet I know that a word can mean so much. Ben is going to write again soon, but today I thought I might give you some news, because he is just now in the midst of a thorough tooth-treatment that makes him often feel miserable, but has to be done now and quickly. Peter has given him a glorious example in having his tonsils out: the whole affair was in the hands of a good doctor, he was only one night in the hospital, no complications, and a general relief. After the tooth-treatment Ben has to undergo the operation too, and we are all convinced that he won't be so subject to malicious grippes, etc. again. In the meantime he has worked very well and very good things, among them a lovely symphony and other works. We all hope that the outward reward will not fail to come but, of course, even in this country queer things happen in the minds of people, they get nation-conscious and forget quite a few of their principles, but I do not think that will ever be very serious and harmful – they are very goodnatured and inclined to reasonable thinking. The country is very beautiful and we make drives along the shore to far points. We had a rather cold spring and now the summer is in full splendour. Amityville *is* a small place by the sea, just the kind of place you advised Ben to go to; he is sitting most of the day on the lawn in front of our cottage. Once in a while we drive to the beach. He has a fine tan and I try to feed him with good things as much as I can . . . good milk, eggs and delicious fruits that are in this country. All his old friends who have not seen him for a while think that he looks splendid. He tells me from your letters how you are, and I am so interested to know about every change in your life. I hope the next weeks will not be too merciless.

Dear Beth, can't you come here or send Sebastian? I had one moment the crazy idea to give you the address of a young friend of mine, of whom I have not heard for months, but who should be due to come to this country. I did not know if it would be pleasant for you in this moment but she is certainly the most reliable person I know, very sweet and young, etc. If you want to approach her or if you want to do it in an emergency, try to locate her mother . . . . This is just a crazy idea in your eyes perhaps, but I thought I might as well tell you. We hope and pray that nothing of the kind is necessary. I have not told Ben about it. B told me that you liked the New Yorker. Tell me if you would like to have something from this country . . . I wish you were all here! . . .

She adds a postscript:

. . . and forgive this rather unconnected letter. I am being interrupted every moment, and – dear – how hard it is to write letters just now, not being able to say the unspeakable things.

Love Elizabeth

We did not actually meet until she came to stay with us on her first visit to England after the war, but after that first letter we corresponded frequently and she sent us wonderful parcels of food and clothes for the children which greatly augmented our sparse rations. When my second child was born she wrote and asked if she could be her god mother, which we were very happy for her to be.

Elizabeth herself had had terrifying experiences before their escape from the Nazis. She told me later what it had been like. They never knew, when there was a knock at the door, if it was to take William, her husband, and the children away to the concentration camps. William had lost his job as a psychiatrist long before, as he was a Jew. The Nazis wanted her to work for them but she would have had to give up William, which she would not do, she kept the family by translating and giving German lessons, until William was offered the post of doctor at the hospital in Amityville, Long Island, and they were able to get away. Her elder daughter, Beata, had left and gone to Italy as nurse some time before, and went from there to the U.S.A. to join the family on their arrival in the States.

Elizabeth found happiness in her new life and met the kind of minds that were her equal; Wystan Auden, Benjamin and Peter among them. It is obvious that she loved Ben from the start and during those ghastly war years, when he was so miserable, homesick and ill, she looked after him like a mother and did her best to take the place of the mother he had lost only three years before.

18

A Japanese Commission and Life with the Mayers

June 11th 1940

Long Island Home
Amityville N.Y.

My darling old Beth,

Your letter came a day or so ago – with all the usual complaints! I'm so sorry, but I hope by now that you have had my long letter with press cuttings, etc. which I sent by boat, (as air-mail is so variable (& expensive!) (these days), & anyhow I have been so terribly busy these last months. My Japanese Symphony [*Sinfonia da Requiem*] has had to be finished – despatched, all in a terrible hurry – & besides I have had lots of sessions with the dentist & you know how that takes up time & energy. I had my awful old front tooth out – & that did the dirty on me – it had an abscess on it, & had what they called a "dry socket" which gave me violent toothache for a fortnight! Nothing serious but you know how I bare pain! However it's all getting better now & soon I shall have a beautiful gleaming smile – like advertisements for Pepsodent! I was glad to hear all your news. It must have been, & still be, absolute hell for you. I'm afraid in this country it has been obvious that things would get to this point, & the complacency of the French and British was rather worrying. However this country was as much to blame not to have helped before – still let's hope that it's not too late now – lots of people think it isn't, thank God. I'm sure one feels out here nearly as bad as you do – because all the news services are so damnably efficient & one feels so terribly helpless – one can't even drive a car and help. However one can talk to people, sign petitions for immediate help to the Allies, & go about & exercise the old charm on people & every little helps to swing public opinion round towards the Allies – and my God, how it has swung since old Chamberlain went! Enough of that. I hope that you are able to do & think, of other things. If there's anything you're short of & I can possibly send, write or cable for it. Even money! I'm terribly grateful for what you're doing re the Mill & Nicholson. I feel so much easier since I knew that you were taking an interest in it. Nicholson is an old fool – never writes – I never know what's happening. I suppose he's disgusted with me – but after all personal opinions shouldn't get in the way of business. However I enclose a cheque (through Peggy Brosa) for any little expenses that may crop up. (Nicholson doesn't send me accounts so I won't send it to him – you might ask to see accounts of Sewell's money or the Craske Div.). Also for anything you or Barbara may be needing – just use your judgement, my darling. It's all I can spare at the moment. My love to you all – hope & pray Kit's still with you – let's all be together soon, somehow! Always thinking of you.

Ben.

June 30th 1940

Long Island Home,
Amityville, NY

My darling Beth, Kit & Sebastian,

I'm writing to you all together because I hope rather superstitiously that it'll mean you are still all 3 together. I don't know how much this evacuation of danger zones has affected you, but to be on the safe side I'll send this to Aunt Julianne to forward. Thank you both for your grand letters. I was delighted to get them. And you, Beth for your cable, saying that you were all right & had got the money – before I forget, talking of money, will you please get in touch with Leslie Boosey, B & H, 295 Regent Street, & get him to send you direct my money – which he can't send to me here. I'm not sure how much it is, but for a start ask for £50, & if it's more I'll let you know. I don't need money at the moment (in fact I'm so rich that I'm going to buy an old Jaloppy for about £20!!) – & I thought that you might be able to use the amount that I'm owed by the firm. I'm writing the same to Barbara, incase this letter miscarries, so don't be disappointed if L. Boosey tells you it's already been sent to her. If you don't need it yourselves perhaps you know of someone who needs it: or Gustel Scherchen may need it to pay transportation fares if they want to send her or Wulff to Canada. Anyhow I want it sent to you rather than to Nicholson as I don't know what he's up to. By-the-way, while we're on the dull subject of business – I don't think there's any sense in selling the Mill at the moment – since its in such a dangerous position & I'm clinging to the hope that one day I'll be able to come back & live there! But I do think we ought to sell the life insurance (as I suggested last year!) so will you tell Nicholson I authorise him to do so. I'll sign.

Of course life here is just hell. I find it impossible to work or think of anything but what you're going through. Every time we have a thunderstorm (& they're pretty bad & frequent here) – I imagine what it must be like in your bombardments. Everyone here takes a gloomy view, of things & rather enjoys being gloomy – that's what makes me so sick. I do hope and pray that you, Beth & Sebastian will soon be able to evacuate yourselves. As I said in my cable I can guarantee your maintenance in this country – & that of any of my young relatives or friends you know of who can get away. Then I'll sign that too. [He signs].

Kit as you are so marvellous with children, have you never thought of applying for a job on one of those Transport ships & looking after kids on this side? It's an idea that struck us. Excuse me if I seem a little over-anxious, but I feel convinced that the more people that get manage away from Europe at the moment, the better. Food shortage everywhere may become a serious problem – & here I am a rich parasite, so why shouldn't I do something to help!

I expect you have all read about America's great swing-over towards the Allies – it's been astonishing, but rather depressing that it needed the fall of Paris to cause it. At the moment it is being rather eclipsed by the fact that the time is come to find a new President – you see the world may be going up in flames (as it seems to be), but nothing must stand in the way of the Americans' political games. It makes one sick. Roosevelt strikes me as being a great man & strangely enough for a man who has ideals, good at the political side too.

At the moment we haven't got many personal plans. Everything is in a state of flux. I don't feel inclined to plan for weeks ahead as no one knows what'll be happening then. So I am going on writing as much as I can; people are just discovering that Peter can sing & he's getting an agent & some jobs. Toni & Peggy are living down here now & it's grand having ones friends around. They're having a difficult struggle I'm afraid since America is a beastly hard country to get going in – & this is just the worst possible moment. But they'll manage to survive, I've no doubt. The Mayers are well – Elizabeth has written to Stella Churchill (an old friend of hers) as she <u>may</u> have some say about Doctors for evaquation of children. I've had beastly trouble with my teeth, but it shows signs of clearing up now. I've also had a boil & a rash – but I'm afraid it's mostly Psychological. I find, as you do too, that if one's mind's upset, that one's body usual[ly] gets that way too. Did I say how much I enjoyed your letters? Please write again if you have time. It's so terrible – the papers only give general news – & never say how people react. The worst side of war never gets into the news. Sebastian sounds a grand kid – I'd give anything to see him again – & you too. Let's pray it'll happen soon. Glad you saw Barbara – must stop this now. Love to all the families – & more than I can say to you three.

Benjamin.

After Dunkirk and the fall of France, with our army back in England, at least what was left of it, there came the fear of invasion by the Nazis. We were less than twenty miles from the coast, and our dear Olga had to leave us, as no aliens were allowed to be within twenty miles of the sea. She was Swiss and she had only three days' notice to go. It was very difficult at such short notice to find a place for her to stay and the only possible place was London. Finally, we found a doctor's family in London who could have her. It was very sad, she did not want to have to leave us. After a few months she was able to return home, which I was glad about, as I felt responsible, having brought her to this country.

Many children were being sent to the United States of America and Kit and I had to think seriously whether to send Sebastian, or whether he and I should go. We had pressing invitations from the Mayers and Ben was also wanting us to go. I did not want to leave Kit and we felt the baby was too young to be sent alone. He was only fifteen months old, so rightly or wrongly we decided to stay together. I was also anxious about Barbara who was in London and was depending on us to be able to get away.

July 26th 1940

c/o Dr. Mayer
123 Louden Avenue,
Amityville
(alias L.I. Home!) N.Y.

My darling Beth,
    It is ages since I heard from you, & I am afraid, ages since I wrote to you – the reasons for the latter are manifold, but the principal reason

is always that I don't know what to write about. I dont know how it affects you to hear of one's normal (un-warlike) doings overhere – if it just makes you vomit, well, just tear the letter up, I'll understand. As a matter of fact, although one is not actually drilling or rolling bandages etc., it would be untrue to say one's life is unwarlike, because everything is clouded by the blasted situation. Although we can go bathing every day – we just can't get up the energy to do it, or enjoy it properly when we do – it's dumb, but there it is! As a matter-of-fact, when we actually did go down to the ocean for the first time the other day, we got such fiendish sun burns (forgetting that the American sun is not so innocent as the English!) that life for a week was hell, & of course we said this was a punishment for enjoying ourselves while you were in agony over the seas. Sadly, but that's another result of war – losing all reasoning powers. Another reason for not writing more often is that I had never before experienced a Long Island summer – and that is saying something. When the temperature is permanently in the 90°'s & humidity is in the 90%'s life is unbearable. One has no energy to do anything, but sit still and even then almost drown in one's perspiration!

I was scared to get your cable until I remembered I'd sent your last letter to Aunt Julianne & the cable was I suppose pointing out that you're still in Swaffham. I'm damn glad, because bad as Norfolk is, to judge by the papers Western cities are not healthy places to be in at this moment. I hope you aren't too bothered by the cable I had to send you – but it had to be arranged, as I don't want the bank to turn nasty and sell the Mill (at a hopeless loss) to redeem my overdraft. . . . . . I don't want anymoney to sit in the Bank doing nothing. Just leave a little to keep the account going & pinch the rest – see? Have a good time yourselves – buy some rum & forget for abit – the same for Barbara! I hereby authorise you to tell Nicholson to do anything you like with my money – [he signs here:] Benjamin Britten he is my attorney so can write cheques – but he himself is hopeless to make decisions. I haven't had a note from him since February.

I've had plenty to occupy myself with recently. The Japanese Government paid up on the dot – & I'm now in contact with the British Embassy in Tokio who wants me to go there in the Autumn to witness the festivities. So I may be leaving for the rising Sun in September – right into the arms of the Mikado – hope he's nice. In the meantime I've been commissioned by a man called Wittgenstein

– a one-armed pianist – to write him a concerto. He pays gold so I'll do it. I bought a cheap car (Ford 1931) for 95 dollars (about £25) – & we now rattle along merrily over the park-ways. It is a 2 seater open (almost the only open car on Long Island!) & though the body is delapidated the engine's fine. We can touch 55 going down hill, if we hold on tight. We've got alot of going about to do in the near future & it's cheaper than train fares.

The Mayer parents have been on holiday these three weeks & Peter & I have been alone here with Michael & Christopher. We see lots of Toni & Peggy (they are very depressed as Toni's big date in Canada to play my Concerto with the Toronto Symphony was cancelled, since he couldn't get an entry visa). Toni & I are working on an orchestral book together for Ralph Hawkes, & it means lots of copying – in which Peggy, Peter & Christopher all join. We haven't been to New York much lately as it's too damned hot – but we were there for a dinner party in our honour last Sunday – an all British party, which sounded gloomy but was quite pleasant after all. We have an invitation to go up into New England next week-end as a result, from the head of the British Board of Commerce in New York – so we're quite official now! A friend of Peter's who is in the Admiralty has arrived here on the purchasing committee, so it's nice to get some first-hand news of England.

I have been having some anxiety over Wulff since I had a letter from Gustel saying he was being shipped to Canada with some other German internees – working it out he should have left England on the day that the Andora Castle went down with hundreds of his kind – so I've been hopping round Red Cross Societies & making inquiries in official circles trying to trace him and to bring some comfort to his poor mother. I had a cable from her this morning saying he missed disaster and arrived here O.K. So I shall now be doing up parcels for him.

Now for a serious word. I do want you all to realise – if by hook or by crook you can get visas to come across, I will guarantee everything this end – if the authorities won't take <u>my</u> guarantee I can <u>easily</u> get you the necessary ones from friends. This goes for any other relatives or friends you know. I've already cabled Sophie [Wyss] to send her kids, but she's "<u>waiting</u>", as if every moment weren't precious – because even if the invasion doesn't come off, life is going to be, if it isn't already, a particularly nasty form of hell; & the more people who can get away the better for everyone. All that has to be done is to arrange for passage & permission <u>your</u> end & I'll do everything here – the government's made it very simple too. I wish to God you three could come – you can't imagine how much I yearn for a sight of the old faces again!

Much love to you all, & be careful (!)

Benjamin

P.S. Please write on only one side of the paper in future –
P.P.S. I have just completed my dental tortures – thank God. I've now got a brand new front tooth which looks as good as – if not much better than (!) – new. <u>Beootiful</u> gold covered with porcelain. I have a wonderful grin. I'm very glad to have that done, but it was bloody expensive!

Benjamin did not go to Tokyo after all in September. I believe the Japanese Government decided that they did not think the *Sinfonia da Requiem* was what they had expected for their Festival; also of course a few months later they attacked Pearl Harbour and were in the war against us.

Barbara was sharing a flat with her friend Helen Hurst in Mallord Street, Chelsea, at that time. When the Blitz started in August 1940, I was very worried about her. I had been in London with Sebastian, staying with the Welford seniors, the night the bombing started, so I knew a bit what it was like. Barbara and Helen decided to stay in their flat rather than go to an air raid shelter, they bought a very strong oak dining table and slept under that.

In Swaffham, with the fear of invasion, there were many obstacles on all the roads to the coast, which made things difficult in getting about, especially for the doctors. The signposts were turned the wrong way and different places put on them, so one had to know the way about or have a map to follow. The air raids were intermittent, but we had them fairly frequently. I joined an ARP group and did duty several times each week.

There was a direct hit on a house in Mallord Street just opposite Barbara's flat, which broke all the flat windows and gave them a terrible shock. That nearly broke Barbara's nerve and she came to stay with us for about ten days. Barbara had always been of an anxious disposition, and I am sure the strain of the London Blitz made her so much worse that she never entirely recovered.

August 25, 1940

Owl's Head Inn, Maine.
As from: Amityville, N.Y.

My darling Beth,

I got your grand long letter about a week ago up here where Peter & I have been staying a week or so having a much needed rest from Amityville – heat & so on. I am delighted that you don't find my letters too unsympathetic & casual in these beastly times, & if you want everyday news you shall certainly have it. Personally it is a relief for me <u>not</u> to write of war, because it is almost the only topic of conversation now, & certainly one thinks about it most of the time. I nearly went dotty during the very bad raids the last week (& as you can guess they are reported pretty "hot" here!), & was overjoyed to get Barbara's cable. So she's away on vacation – that's fine – wish she could stay out of London altogether. Your & Kit's letters I may point out have been <u>grand</u> – it has been very illuminating the way the war has been reflected in people's letters – & I'm damn proud the way my family has come out of it. Of course you can't help showing you're depressed now & then, Barbara too, poor dear – but you three (B.B. & K.) have kept your integrity marvellously. Robert's letters have changed since Wellingboro' – full of scandals & school affairs (most amusing – I enjoyed it no end) & only a slight patriotic peroration at the end. Lennox – poor dear – all brave. Sophie – sweet, all bound up in Music & children. Enid Slater – just desparate, she doesn't seem to have anyone to talk to much. The most depressing is Ethel Bridge, who has gone wildly flag-waving & bloodthirsty – I just dread her letters. Still she is probably in the happiest state, living where she is. Frank is more balanced. And so on – very interesting, if one weren't so emotionally hit by it all. This is all to point out how very much your letters are appreciated! Please continue.

Thank you most awfully for looking after the money side of my things – I feel relieved to know you are doing it. I at last had a letter from Nicholson saying nothing in particular rather distractedly. Poor dear, having to run that business without much help. Anyhow I signed a form authorising him to sell life insurance & telling him to send you the residue (if any) after paying off the overdraft. And don't bother to put my money on deposit unless you really want to – because I want you consider it the money as yours & <u>nothing</u> to do with me – none of this keeping some incase of future. <u>If</u> I come back I'll come back with enough (D.V.W.P.! [*Deo volens* (God willing), weather permitting] to live on. So – don't go asking my permission to buy a new coat – buy 20 if there's enough money. I'm glad you could pay Barbara's bill for telephone. Does she need any more? Oh dear, oh dear I do feel so bad that I can't send any more – but I daren't because now B & H can't pay me any more here I have to rely on commissions & they aren't very frequent – & poor Peter's jobs aren't coming in very fast as yet. But if there is any urgent need – cable & I can get money easily; you've no idea of my resources!!!

Well, Peter is telling you all about our trip up here & the adventures with the little green Ford (blast it). I shall be sorry to leave to-morrow, altho' our holiday isn't over yet, as we are going to stay with Wystan in the Berkshire mountains (Massachusetts). Get out your map & see where we are – 200 miles from Canadian border – right on the ocean. A grand spot – but sea is too cold for comfortable bathing. Rock-land is nearest town – & Portland nearest big place (150 miles S.W. of us). I don't know how long we shall be in Massachusetts – all depends on weather & money. I have been busy up here & finished all the sketches for my latest commission (the one-handed piano concerto for Wittgenstein); but I still have lots of things to get done. Good thing to be busy – & so far the ideas come rolling in. Then I suppose we shall go back to Amityville for abit – at anyrate until I've had my old tonsils out – which will be as soon as my throat is fit. Incidentally ask Kit if he knows about the great Sulfa's – Sulfamilamide and Sulfapyridine – which are all the rage here now & judging by accounts amazingly successful. One is for pneumonia & one for Streptococcic infections – I can't remember which is which. I know that I had one of them last week & certainly it brought down my temp, which was round about 103° on Sat. evening to 98.7° on Sunday morning! And the Dr. Brown who attended me has had some staggering results with the pneumonia one. Wish we had had it in 1937! They've only been out here for about a year, but apparently were invented in Europe & not much used for a long time. Anyhow – nice to think of people inventing things to save lives nowadays! I expect to have tonsilectomy at the beginning of September – & I expect I shall go on living in Amityville, for when Christopher goes back to school & Michael takes an apartment (American for "flat") in New York instead of "commuting" (going up & down in a train to N.Y. everyday!) & as Ulli has as job & Beata will be living in New York the parents will be lonely & press us to stay with them – & certainly it is very cheap to do so. Actually one gets abit tired of it – you see the Home is really a small village where everyone knows everyone & everyone's business, & the intrigues & scandals are unbelievable. Dr. Mayer gets very tired of the work too – he had his own practice in Munich, & it is difficult for him not being the boss. Dr. Titley, the boss, is a younger man, not such a fine psychiatrist, but a good organiser & there is a certain amount of friction – & of course it is the old story about the <u>wives</u> of all the doctors, and asking the staff to meals – <u>this</u> person sulks because <u>that</u> person has been asked twice a week & she has only been asked once. Not that lots of the people aren't nice, but it seems impossible for people to be shut up together without squabbling. And Mrs. Mayer, darling as she is, is inclined to put people's backs up by not being tactful; of course she is very intelligent & has met lots of poets & writers & can speak six languages, but that doesn't excuse her in the eyes of the assistant-secretary who has been snubbed for talking of the new doctor's lady-friend – etc. etc. etc. So it's all abit trying. Luckily Mrs. Titley (who is also a doctor & practises in the home) is one of the most charming people I've ever met, & she makes life well bearable there, altho' she herself has a packet of trouble. This has been a tough year with innumerable crises – the Long Island home crises (mostly acutely emotional!) are famous – & she has come out tops every time. I'm longing for you to meet these people. God how I hope you come over here – or I bring them over to England – the Mayers & the Titleys are well worth knowing! Peter & I are (when we are there) living with the Mayers now – we slept at the Titley's house for about 8 months & eat at the Mayers – shucks! I'd better draw you a map of the place:

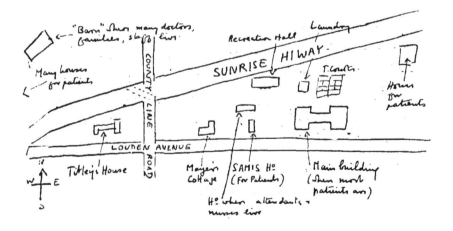

154

The pencil is the road system actually on the grounds – the ::: is a tunnel under the Sunrise Hiway (American for Highway!). The County Line Road divides Nassau from Suffolk county – actually the county line goes through the Titley's house & the East being Suffolk – we have been sleeping in Suffolk all the time.

Everything is done very well in the place of course. The arrangement about food is that cooking is done in the actually (sic) houses & cottages individually, but the food is bought by the central Main building & distributed from there, & paid for by the Home! Servants – Titleys have three & a nurse for Rachel (aged 4). Mayers – one, a black (actually coffee-coloured) – Edith – abit clumsy & slap-dash (slap-*dish* would be more appropriate!) but with a heart of gold & never gets upset although ten visitors may arrive unexpectedly for dinner – which often happens! So you see, apart from little extras (such as Coca-Cola – the american national drink – made from a Cola-bean, which is not immediately attractive, but is a slight stimulant, and grows on one lots!) we don't <u>cost</u> the Mayers anything. So our consciences are easy on that – & both Doctor and Mrs. M. <u>do</u> seem to like having us; at least when we go away they write & say they miss us & want us back quickly! Actually Peter ought to be more in New York next season, so we'll have to see whether we can afford a room for him somewhere & I'll go on living at Amityville. But it seems hopeless to try & make plans – one can only speculate these days. It has been fun having Peggy & Toni living in Amityville too, & as Wystan often comes down, & Ralph Hawkes too, we have been quite a colony. People still seem to like the English here – at least one's accent makes people prick their ears up, even if they don't understand a word! You've no idea how difficult it is to make people understand often – especially in shops – & quite often people think you're being snooty – which I don't like being considered – even if its true! But on the whole people envy us being English – altho' we have made such a goddam mess of our politics – though the American system is pretty lousy too.

Thank you so much for the photos which I carry about with me in my pocket book. Sebastian looks a grand kid, I'd love to see him! Give him a pat where he likes it best from Uncle Ben! I'm sorry you didn't like my picture. <u>I</u> thought it rather impressive, although the wind was doing its damnedest that day, I remember. Certainly the garb was yankee – but rather comfortable, & people wear most highly coloured stuff over here, you know. And, by general consent, brushing my hair <u>slightly</u> back (<u>not</u> right back) instead of only sideways, helps matters by giving me a forehead, which I didn't have much of before. Of course now with my new tooth I've got a real Kolynos grin. Anyhow I've got to have some nice press photos taken soon & then I'll send you some to judge.

I must stop this screed. The trouble is (don't laugh) that I take up so much time writing to you & Barbara that I don't write to anyone else – so I get numerous bitter complaints from other sources. . . .

Much love to you all three. Even if the invasion <u>doesn't</u> come, do still try & come over – this winter isn't going to be much of a picnic – to be avoided it possible. Anyway remember that if there is the slightest chance & you want something done this end, just cable & it'll be done. Why I said just write on one side of the page was because censors have a habit of cutting bits out of your letters & when you write on both sides I lose <u>two</u> sections of interesting news not only one. See? So please get <u>thin</u> paper. I'm in touch with Wulff who is safely in Canada & seems in not too bad a way. Thank goodness he <u>is</u> over here now. Best place for him.

Much love my darling, write again & often,

Ben.

P.S. Beata, who's here with us sends her love. Peter hasn't completed his saga of our trip & will send it in a day or so.   Love B.

19

More Letters from America – Future Plans

Letter from Peter

As from Amityville   Owl's Head Inn
August 25th 1940 [finished Sept. 18th]   Owl's Head, Maine.

My dear Beth

I've been meaning to write to you for a long time, partly because it may interest you to get another angle on your little brother's goings on, and partly to congratulate you on your letters (you and Kit) which Ben had passed on to me to read, I hope you don't mind. I must say I hope everyone reacts to the war as you seem to have done – it's impressive – but I am afraid they don't. My mother is allright, but my father, whenever I express some concern for their safety, accuses me of being influenced by Nazi propaganda! <u>You</u> make life sound still worth living and do something to counteract the radio and newspapers here. Your infant sounds adorable – I wish I had seen him when he was a little older than that very young thing I met in Hallam Street once. Come over here, all of you. You'd like it where we are now, I think. We couldn't bear the heat and humidity of Long Island any longer (when we left it was 99° and humidity 100% if that means anything to you!) and so Ben bought a 2-seater 1931 Ford for 95$ (is that the right sign?) and after preliminary runnings around Amityville, and particularly to Jones beach, a long flat semi-island covered with sand-dunes and reeds a bit like Essex, where I lost the ignition key in the sand and Wystan Auden had to hitch-hike 5 miles to the station to catch a plane to California, we started to "Journey North!". The car is green and looks battered under its make-up – the hood is marvellously porous, lets every drop in, but the tyres (they call them shoes here!) are superb (we have 2 spares) ... (notice the past tense). We planned to spend a weekend at the Berkshire

Festival (Koussevitsky and the Boston Symph.) with Aaron Copland, before we came on up to Maine (in all about 500 miles, carrying a very heavy load; Peggy and Toni in the Dicki supported innumerable Brosa suitcases and a violin, with a trunk strapped on at the side and Ben and me in front wearing all our clothes, to avoid packing them. We started at 6 am, and all was well till we stopped for lunch, and then came the first rebellious symptoms. She went, but unwillingly, and we hoped it was just after-dinner wind (do you remember the woman at Burleigh House?). Alas, she stopped the next afternoon on the way to the Festival. It was hot, and you know how popular old green Fords are when they hold up a hundred Cadillacs – Ben almost died with shame. I went to get a breakdown van, the man was out, and of course when I finally brought him back in a van after 20 minutes, Ben had just managed to start the car. A garage took her to pieces and put her together again; so did another one the next day, when she stopped after going five miles, downhill. All the mechanics were mystified; there was nothing wrong with her. No sooner had they said this than the car proceeded to go a hundred miles in perfect order. The next day we dropped Peggy and Toni off at Cape Cod and drove up here by easy stages. But you can imagine what Ben's nerves were like driving for 300 miles when you never knew when you might stop! He had to stop at every comfort station we passed!

Williamsburg, Massachusetts. Sorry I meant to finish this screed and enclose it with Ben's letter but somehow I never got down to it. Well, we left Owl's Head in fairly good order, having had new valves put in the day before – That was expensive enough – but after going 150 miles she suddenly had a short & the lights went out and the car stopped, luckily at a garage, but of course one tyre was flat too – Really, who would buy an old car? They are nothing but trouble and strife – Then that garage turned out to be run by college boys, who threw themselves gallantly head foremost under the bonnet, but only made more trouble inside; And so on. Eventually we got where we wanted to go, to a place called Essex, near a town called Ipswich (it was rather like East Anglia!). Maine was lovely, rather like a mixture of Scotland and Austria. Here, it's much more like England, but everything's on such an enormous scale, that when you say this is like England, it's really like a particular piece of England multiplied by twenty. The whole of England and Scotland is smaller than New

York State! It's fantastic! People in this part of the States are much more Anglo-Saxon, all the children in Rockland were blond, few coloured people at all even in the towns; it's very different further south & around New York. We're staying on a farm, where Wystan Auden has been spending the summer, it's all very like an English farm – the Cotswolds, except that they make most of their money from corn (Indian) and maple sugar.

Amityville. I'm terribly sorry, Beth, I just don't seem to be able to finish this letter. This time it was all the news of the London bombings, which made me hold my breath and sit close to the radio. I had a letter from my father yesterday from London, posted on the 6th, the day before the bad bombings began. I hope to God they're still allright – Is Barbara still in London?

We had a very nice time with Wystan and then stayed some days with a friend near there. She had a lovely house, with lots of records, and many so-called "Primitive" American paintings i.e. colonial eighteenth century stuff. She had a wonderful cook too and fed us very well. But it was rather high up in the hills and cold and Ben caught an awful cold which he has still got, although back here it's very warm. It was lovely to be back again with the Mayers, they are such marvellous people.

I hope Ben will have his tonsils out some time very soon. They've been a perfect pest all summer. Then he and Wystan and I have taken an apartment in New York or rather Brooklyn, with a lovely view over the river. I know Ben will hate it, he loathes New York anyway, but he must be on the spot sometimes to meet people and he can always come down here if he wants to.

I'm trying to decide when and if to come back to England. I had a stinking letter from a cousin of mine Steuart Wilson, who has got out here a very good job that he's not leaving, but thinks by Gad Sir! that I ought to be back doing my duty. I don't know whether to come or wait till everyone's called back. One will have to face a lot of criticism over here meanwhile – Everyone's getting more and more militant, and a lot of people think U.S. will be in the war by the New Year.

What do you think about it? Shall I come?

Much love to you all

Peter.

I wrote back to Peter and said I thought it would be better to come – they would have to in the end, and I felt it better they should come at their own free will.

September 18th 1940

Amityville, N.Y.

My darling Beth, & Kit, & Sebastian,

This is only a scribbled note to put in with Peter's, as it is late & I want to go to bed, but didn't like to send his off without a word. Your letter Kit has just arrived; thank you more than I can say. It was a grand description, & gave me a very vivid picture of what you are going through. My God, if I could only get you out of it all. I'm praying that something will materialise out of our scheme, but I've had no news from Dr. Churchill as yet. If anything whatever occurs don't hesitate to come as I can always get friends to guarantee your existance – see? That of course goes for Barbara too. Where is she? Surely not in London still? Can't you persuade her to leave. Sorry if this is all hysterical (& out of date when it arrives probably) but all one can think of at the moment is the News, & that is pretty ghastly. I'm afraid I've got very bad wind-up, probably much worse than you all have – but it's only not hearing from you, and not having an idea of what's happening to you.

We got back here the day-before-yesterday, & it is grand to be back with the family again. They are such dears & such a comfort in these bloody times. Peter & I are going to take a flat with Wystan Auden for the winter in Brooklyn – one of the districts of New York City. We feel we have to be nearer the big city where things go on & jobs are born. But I loathe the idea of living in a town again – I expect I shall always be hopping down to Amityville again. The flat ("apartment" here) is quite nice – bit small – with a grand view of the river, which is something. It is very cheap by New York standards – but hideously expensive by English & the current exchange) – nearly £5 a week! It's a terribly dear place to live in. Luckily all parts of America are not the same.

There are lots of problems to be settled at this moment & it is very worrying. There are so many alternatives as to what to do, & what one <u>wants</u> to do too – that I, who never was good at decisions, don't know where I am. I wish to God I could be back with you, but that's

160

no use, because obviously if I were back I couldn't be <u>with</u> you – so that's not much sense. One feels bad about not suffering as well & of course many militant people here are very cross with us for being alive at all (esp. old ladies) – but one must try & be realistic, & that's what I'm trying to work out now – where one is most use and least bother. If you have any ideas let me know! (Officially one must stay put).

By-the-way I was horrified to find that the selling of the Life Insurance didn't cover the overdraft, Beth. If the Boosey and Hawkes money doesn't cover it from next quarter (i.e. if they can pay at all, which I doubt) – you'd better let me know. But at the moment I'm a bit broke & can't send any – what with the new tooth in front, my tonsils, the blasted car that would go wrong & now the flat! I wish I could sell that Mill.

I must stop now my dears. All luck to you.

Keep your heads – & don't get caught by any emotional hulla balloos ("duty" & what not) – but I know you will.

Much, much love to you all
Ben

Kit and I did not try and persuade Ben to sell the Mill, although at that time none of us could use it much. We should have had to sell at a great loss as it was in such a dangerous position near the coast, or the army would probably have taken it over. We three, Barbara, Kit and I, went there when we could and somehow kept the place going, for which we were glad later, when Snape for some years became a sanctuary for us all.

Late in 1940 Kit was called up. We spent Christmas at Peasenhall with the Welford seniors, the last Christmas they were to be there. In 1941 the Welfords let the place to the Land Army and moved to Bromeswell near Woodbridge.

Kit was centred in London, examining air crews. We wanted to be together, but it seemed mad to take the baby to London with the Blitz going on, so we found a house in Northwood, Middlesex, within commuting distance of London but just far enough away to avoid the worst of the bombing. The good thing about the place was that Barbara and Helen could also commute and so get some relief. The house was large enough to house us all, plus two maids. It seems incredible now that I should have had two maids living in, in a house not so very large.

May 12th 1941

My darling, darling old Beth,

Your very sweet latter arrived just now – as, believe it or not, I was just about to take up a pen to break the long silence. I was terribly glad to get it & to know that you are still all right – that means I shall have a few moments relief from anxiety about you until something else happens to start me worrying again! I am delighted that you have got Barbara away from London, at anyrate for the nights – I have been on tenter hooks about her being in that bloody inferno all this time. I hope it isn't too tiring for her to "commute" (American word, meaning – "to go backwards and forwards by train or bus to a large town to work" – convenient, isn't it?!) every day. And I am also delighted that Kit can see you so often. It would have been hell for you to go through all this & never see him. I hope he's not too unhappy about his work – he is still <u>medical</u>, isn't he? I mean, he doesn't have to fly – just tend broken legs, etc. . .?? Some day – some day – I shall be able to get you over here & he'll do work he really likes, in a small place, near the sea & miles away from noise, fashion & sophistication & all the things he hates. I am feeling like that too now. A winter in New York is just about the limit for me – especially in these times when everyone is so het up & panicky – you can't imagine how hysterical Americans can be – especially in places like New York. If the British Navy sink a ship – the war is won; – if a British General is captured – then there's no sense in going on with the war, better give it up. When one is feeling racked because of family & friends in bombardment, & with the anxiety & hard labour in trying to establish a reputation in a new, & not particularly friendly country, it's just about as much as one can take. However I have very good friends & of course Amityville I can flee to, if it gets too much for me – such as this present moment.

I am afraid one of the reasons that I've been so long in writing is not that I have been occupied <u>every</u> waking moment (I know you wouldn't believe me if I said I have been!), but that I haven't had the time to settle down to the kind of letter that was worth writing to you after the long gap.

Now I have got this one off my chest I am going to write short letters more frequently, and not always by air-mail, because it is so expensive. I am delighted that you liked my Violin Concerto. I gather that it was a pretty bad performance – by the notices & by Ralph Hawkes' account. How I wish you could have heard Toni do it with the New York Philharmonic – that is really something! I was sent most of the notices & was surprised that they were so good – because after all they might easily be sour about me being able to go on working regardless of everything. I am glad you'd the feeling that I have "grown up" – well, may be I have at last! If I haven't with all this, I don't think there's much chance of me ever doing so! I think I look more or less the same – I'm not going bald as someone (Barbara I think) suggested – merely brushing my hair further back instead of across. Gives me a fine forehead – that's why! I must see if I can get a photo to send you – maybe I have one in New York, only there's been rather a run on them recently, with all the performances that have been occuring.

Well, I have produced my first Symphony (the Requiem one, in memory of Mum and Pop, paid for by the Japanese Government – nice touch that – don't you think?) & my first opera. Neither could be called an unqualified success, but the reaction was everywhere violent which I suppose is a good thing, but personally I hate it. I'd much rather it was praised mildly everywhere – I feel embarrassed at being the subject of animated debate. Roughly speaking – the reaction of the public has been excellent – in every case much applause (three or four calls for me at each performance of the Symphony) – the reaction of the intellectual composers has been bad (I am definitely disliked (a) because I am English (no music ever came out of England) (b) because I'm not American (everything is nationalistic), (c) because I get quite alot of performances (d) because I wasn't educated in Paris – etc. etc.) – the reaction of the press mixed – usually the respectable papers (like the Times) bad or puzzled – the rag papers or picture papers good – funny, isn't it? The opera "Paul Bunyan" I think you'd like alot – full of tunes that people even whistle! – and it's quite good entertainment, but the labour involved was enormous – a whole evening's work is no joke to write and score, let alone supervise the rehearsals. The performance wasn't too good, but there are future productions in sight, which may be better. Besides this I have conducted three concerts with my Riverhead orchestra, which were strenuous but not altogether unrewarding; they are so enthusiastic, although not exactly efficient. I may go on next season – if they can raise the money to keep it up. I hope so, because in a way I feel it is doing something tangible in return for the hospitality of the country. I have also written several articles for periodicals, with great effort, & with the aid of Peter and Wystan over grammar and spelling! Peter is singing "<u>Les Illuminations</u>" (first performance in America) over the Radio on Sunday afternoon – & if I can get permission from the Unions (the great new American racket at the moment) I shall conduct. I have also written a large two-piano piece, [*Introduction and Rondo Alla Burlesca op 23 no. 1,* written Nov 21st 1940] for Ethel Bartlett & Rae Robertson, which they play from time to time. So you see I've been occupied, which is a blessing these days. I hope your reaction to all this nonsense won't be aggravation, which I could easily understand tho! I know, compared with what is happening everywhere, all this has little importance – but I feel that it is the only thing I can do well, and after all music does give alot of comfort to those not actually in the firing line as you are – infact it's quite extraordinary how music is flourishing at the moment, & agents tell me that bookings are going wonderfully for next year, when everyone knows America will be in the war. That by the way is the general opinion. There is still a great deal of anti-war feeling but Roosevelt is being very cunning in being just sufficiently far ahead of public opinion, but not too far so as to be over thrown & some reactionary quasi-fascist power be put in instead.

Our plans for the summer are of course abit vague – but Peter & I have had an invitation to go to spend some time in South California (with Ethel and Rae Robertson) & as we want to go to Mexico so as to get on to the labour-quota (you have to go out of the country & then come back, so as to be able to work without hindrance) that all fits in well. I also have a great deal of work to get done, & if possible I want to land a Holywood job – and then how rich we'll all be – I shall be able to send you lots of money! That, quite seriously, is the only reason I want to make money – so that you can live a little easier & have the little creature comforts that make life abit more bearable. I'll see about the parcels of food, but the boats don't go very often so don't expect it too soon, will you?

I feel bad about my God-son – but perhaps in a few years it will be a good thing to have a rich uncle in America (who knows!)

May 13 I meant to have finished this yesterday, but I had to leave to go & play in a concert (2 piano duets with an American composer called McPhee) where Peter was conducting his choral society. It went very well & there was much animated applause . . . & promises of future dates, which may or may not materialise. However, one lives on promises these days.

I am just about to leave for Brooklyn by train (about an hour away). I have a lot of business to do in the city & I shall stay a few nights in our house there – the house that Peter, Wystan & I share with a man called George Davis (one of the editors of Harper's Bazzaar). It is quite nice & convenient, tho' a trifle too bohemian for my liking – I like the ordinary dull routine more & more, the older I get! I can't live wildly <u>and</u> work! I don't think your brother would shock you, my dear, if you met him. He is still quite a sober, God-fearing person – and altho' you never believe it, he <u>does</u> work pretty hard! But he only lives for the day when he can meet his sisters and bro.-in law and nephew – whom he thinks of continually, altho' he fails to write as often as he should. Please forgive me, my darling old Beth, but I have been horribly busy. Please tell Barbara that I'll write in a few days, but I'm going to send this right away without waiting – Much love to Kit & Dopey. Just had a nice letter from Peter Welford & Piers Dunkerley. All my love, my dear. Bear up – le diable est mort!

Ben

July 6th 1941

Route 1 Box 345,
Escondido,
California.

My darling old Beth,

Your letter arrived yesterday morning, & I was so glad to get it – not that I can say it was seven months since I heard, but it was fully three! Actually, although I know I have been sadly dilatory, it isn't quite as long as that since I wrote, because I know I wrote (by Airmail, too) at least twice since Christmas – one describing the concert in N. York when Bartlett & Robertson played my piece, and another about the Brooklyn flat – but they went astray somewhere I suppose – like the parcels of food I sent the Bridges & Peter sent his mother. It is sickening, but these are the consequences of this present bloody period of history. How I wish I were born in another time – when things weren't universally so bloody.

Well, Peter & I continue to have a nice time out here – it is pretty hot, but the house remains cool & the ocean is fairly near. I have been working pretty hard, and shall not have much unoccupied time this summer, I can see – what with Mrs. Coolidge's new commission [*String Quartet No 1*] & the odd concertos I have to write for people. However I'm not complaining – it's damned lucky to have work to do, & to be able (so far) to do it. Peter is working hard at his singing, & singing like a real opera star, very loud & high. The ocean bathing (I'm afraid this must make your mouths water, poor dears) is lovely, with surfing; but the latter isn't nearly as good as Cornwall was. The rollers are big, but not nearly so long. The Pacific doesn't look any different from the Atlantic, you know, & certainly tastes the same. The fish that come out of it aren't as good as the North Sea – take it from me – & I'd give anything for a good Kipper! The Pacific is full of battleships & what-not, & the air full of aeroplanes – San Diego, the big naval base, is near here – & one sees as many uniforms about almost as in England. I know it (this apparent American indifference) must seem infuriating to you all, but Roosevelt is being very smart. You see, this is such an enormous country, & takes such a long time to move – Europe seems so far off from the Middle-West or West – Roosevelt is just moving a little ahead of public opinion all the time, & that is gradually swinging round to realisation that something's got to be done. After all England & France took a long time to make up their minds about Spain, Austria etc. – but there's no doubt that America will be "in" it before very long. The real trouble is the Nazi-influence in South America, which is really dangerous. No more of that – I expect you get as sick of News-commentators as we do. Now, we hardly ever listen to the wireless – one always seems to hear what news there may be sooner or later, & it's no use going all of a flap every five minutes with hysterical news revues.

Its so grand to think of you all living together. I suppose that Barbara & Helen will be with you permanently now they've had to give up the flat. I'm glad that you are O.K. financially – but if anything goes wrong & you want any little things that make life more worth living, don't hesitate to write or cable for it. It can always be raised however large! Please give the enclosed letters to Barbara & Helen. Please tell everyone who complains that I'll write sooner or later, but I've got so many letters to write & if I write I want to write to you! Much love my darling. P.T.O.

Give my love to Kit & Sebastian – he does sound a grand kid; how I wish I could see him. I hope Kit isn't too down about the job he's got to do, but impress on him that it's only temporary & that all bad things come to an end. I am regarding this only as a period of marking-time, & living for the future which will be the same as it was always, with us all together either there or here! Much love again, my darling. Bear up. Love to the Welfords when you see them –

Ben.

I do hope I've got your address right, but it's somewhat obscurely written – it looks like GATEHUGS to me, but that's too good to be true.

I shall be at this address until at anyrate the end of August – so write here direct will you, please?

June 17th 1941

My darling old Beth

Just a note in Barbara's to say hullo, and how I've not forgotten you (altho' have you forgotten me by your long silence?), and how the next letter will be a long one to you & one to Kit. I've been very busy on a string quartet for Mrs. Coolidge to be done in a rush and we have to go to Los Angeles for a few days to see some people – but when I get back, I'll write. There hasn't been any news – Barbara 'll tell you what there has been. I'm so pleased that the last few months have been a respite for you in the way of bombings & bad news – <u>maybe</u> something good will happen at last, & then what a time we'll have. How's Sebastian – he must be growing enormous now. How much can he say now? I hope the house arrangement is a success & that things are working out alright. Things are fine here – mostly just hard work, and occasional excursions to the beach. I'm very brown (the Californian sun <u>is</u> powerful!) and putting on weight – I have nearly reached the 10 stone mark again!

All the best my dear.

Take care of yourself & write soon.   Love.

Ben.

August 19th 1941 Escondido

Escondido
(but please send letters to
Amityville in the future)

My darling old thing,

I have been carrying this paper around for three hectic days in Hollywood, hoping to get a chance to write to you, but, not surprisingly considering what that place is like, it didn't materialise. However, when I got back here there was a letter from you waiting for me, & so I can answer it, & also say thank you very much for it. I was getting a wee bitty worried since you usually write so regularly, so I was relieved as well as pleased to get it, & such a nice long one too! Heavens, how I wish I could see you all again – goodness knows when that'll be. But actually, for the first time for years one has almost been able to look ahead – since the incredible Russian resistance, & also America's waking up to facts at last. In fact Washington's official opinion is that Germany is beaten & knows it – but I'm abit scared that in going down she may drag so many others down with her. God grant that a great man may arise who can organise a better kind of peace than 1918. Please excuse the digression into politics, but everyone talks them & one can read nothing else but long prophecies, usually completely false. Actually I am short-sighted enough only to worry about the present, & can only be happy when those I love aren't living a hell-on-earth existance.

By the way, old thing, please forgive me if this letter is a little more disjointed & stupid than usual, because I'm writing it in the heat of a Californian afternoon (& that's <u>something</u> I can tell you, it was 90° in the shade a few hours ago!) – and also Ethel & Rae are practising downstairs & if anything is more disturbing than one piano it's two. Life is going on much the same as usual here with occasional excursions into Hollywood – to concerts that Barbirolli conducts at The Bowl, and to see odd people that are, have been, or may be useful to any of us. It is an extraordinary place – absolutely mad, and really horrible. I can't really attempt to describe it, because it has no relation to any other place on earth. It actually isn't a place by itself but a suburb of Los Angeles, which is the ugliest and most sprawling city on earth. The chief features of Hollywood are that the things that one worries about so much don't matter a damn – money, time, distance, behaviour, clothes, (especially for men). It is completely unreal. Peter

& I stayed with friends – enormously rich, altho' they have only average jobs. One house we stayed in was built like a boat, with a moat round it – & in the middle of all the other houses – which anyhow are any and every stile from a native mud-hut to an Indian temple – via Pagodas & Spanish villas – it would drive Mr. Welford mad! The driving is mad – I saw a wonderful little argument between 2 cars – the one on the right wanting to go left across the other which wouldn't give way. After blowing its horn madly for about 1 minute (they were both travelling about 45 down a main Boulevard), it started to swerve madly about – like this [diagram] until finally it just barged straight into the side of the other, & there was an awful crash – just because neither could give way! Typical of all Hollywood driving – & Peter & I had enough of it, because as no distance one ever goes is less than 5 miles, one is driving all the time! As amatter of fact, one has to get just as hard as the other drivers, although I didn't go so far as crashing cars I didn't like!

I am glad Kit seems to be liking his job more, & that you got away for abit of leave. How are the Welfords? I feel rather bad about not having written for so long – but I have been so really terribly busy, & the only time one gets for letter-writing is after dinner, & something about the California air & sun makes me so tired then. Please tell Barbara I'll write to her in a few days, but I don't want this to wait any longer. By-the-way would you please send the enclosed to Who's-Who for me – I'm about a year late already with it! I feel so embarrassed with this sort of thing – they are alright for film-stars or politicians, but poor old hack composers have such dull lives, & nothing to fill books with!

Peter & I are probably going East again in a few weeks – when I get the present work finished – lots of things one can't do by letter have got to be done – & also, frankly, I'm abit sick of California – there is a feeling of unreality about it which is not so pleasant as you'd think! My dear, how I should love to speak to you on the telephone – but anyhow even when it is not so expensive, it's not allowed for private people at the moment (Wystan raised heaven & earth to be allowed to when his mother was ill, to no avail). But I have a feeling that we'll be together again sooner than we think – I don't know why I'm feeling so hopeful to-day, pray something awful hasn't happened by the time you get this.

My love to Kit & the child – he sounds marvellous now, but if he grows up like his mother he'll even improve I know! Love to Barbara & Helen and lots to yourself, old thing – I'm always thinking about you!

Ben.

20

Meeting with Koussevitsky

November 4th 1941

Long Island Home, Amityville, N.Y.

My darlingest Beth,

I am so dreadfully sorry not to have written for so long but since I wrote last things have been really hectic. First of all there was all the business of leaving California, which was complicated by Rae Robertson having a smash in the car and all the repairs had to be done before we could leave, and also I had a concert in Los Angeles when my quartet (for Mrs. Coolidge) was first-performed, and Peter's & my journey back had to start from there. I won't bore you with all the millions of details about all these things, & I'll try to stick to the main items. [. . .]

The journey back was very pleasant – we motored of course and took about ten days, staying with friends here & there & taking a rather devious course as a result. But at the beginning we went pretty fast, about 2300 miles in 4 days! When I got back here I had to sit down at once & write an overture for a conductor here – it had to be done in a great hurry, and I'm afraid (again, between you & me!) I didn't do an awfully good job – it is so difficult to think clearly sometimes these days. However it'll pass muster for the moment, & I hope to rewrite it sometime. That done – I had to go off to Boston to see Koussewitsky & hear the Boston Orchestra rehearse my Requiem Symphony which they & he are playing this year in Boston & New York. As you know, from records, they are the most wonderful orchestra and played it marvellously – so I was thrilled to pieces. This piece of news is the best thing that's happened to me here so far – because it has the best propaganda value – to have them play ones work in New York – so congratulate me!!

The next thing to occupy me (and to make letter writing difficult) was a fuss about Papers – and in these times that is no joke, because the amount of red-tape is terrible. Actually it was Peter who was directly concerned, but having similar papers to him I was hauled in as an example. It caused a terrific lot of letters – & finally a journey down to Washington to see unpleasant officials. Luckily, owing mostly to Mrs. Mayer who knows all the "right" people and seems always able to get one out of tight spots, it was put straight – & anyhow the journey to Washington wasn't only on that account since I had my "medal" to receive. This was at the Library of Congress and was presented by Mrs. Coolidge for "eminent services to chamber-music"!! It was quite an alarming ceremony, but Mrs. Coolidge, who is really a sweet old thing, made things easier by publicly referring to me as "Benjy", which made everyone smile sweetly! The Coolidge Quartet played my quartet with quite good success. We got back late on Friday last – this week-end Thomas Matthews (whom you heard play my violin concerto) & his wife were here on a visit – they are simple & nice people, on their way to Singapore. Yesterday I spent most of the day in New York on business – seeing my agent about things (*possibly* a commission from Benny Goodman!) – which brings me to to-day, & is, I hope a good enough excuse for not having written before – but I'm sorry, my dear, & promise to be better in future.

Thank you so very much for your lovely letters & the 'photos – I am terribly proud of my nephew & show him to everyone with pride – I was also delighted with the picture of you, not exactly prepossessing, but very typical, with cigarette & frown!!! I had to use all my Britten fortitude to keep from spilling a tear or two. Gosh, what I'll do when I see you I can't think – probably be quite dumb & not be able to think of anything to say (which usually happens on such occasions)! About the question of America & Kit after this bloody war – I have inquired and <u>every</u> place you go to to become a Doctor, I'm afraid you have to take a medical exam. I don't know how hard it is, although the Americans have a reputation of being rather advanced medically. However I know quite a few doctors who have passed, it so I'm sure Kit could. But I shouldn't dream of coming unless you could bring some money out (which will probably be easy after the war), because there are hideous stories of doctors all qualified who can't find work & are starving. Anyhow, wait & see what the position is – maybe I'll be so rich that I can support you all! Consider it tho', because America I should think will be the place after the war, & I can arrange all the necessary papers for you. Damn – I'm on the 4th page & I want to put one in for Barbara. Excuse the abrupt finish – but you know what I feel about love and wishes & all that, so please take lots & lots of love for granted to you all from your devoted bro.

Ben

Frank Bridge died on January 10th, which was a great sadness to Benjamin, especially as he was not able to be with him at the last, and had not seen him since May 1939 when Ben left for the States.

During the summer of 1941, we carried on pretty happily at "Gatehouse", Northwood with Kit going to London each weekday, and Barbara and Helen arriving each night: two little brown ladies with little brown suitcases – they were both small, and seemed to wear brown a lot. Kit told us funny stories of some of the hopefuls he had to examine. Half of them were illiterate, could barely write their names.

The bombing on London started to ease up later that summer, the Nazis having probably realised that however hard they tried they could not break the cockney spirit. The fear of invasion seemed to be not so imminent as before, as the Germans had turned their attack on Russia. Barbara and Helen's flat had been repaired, so they came down to us less often. In September Kit and I managed to get away for a weekend to Cambridge, which was bliss. We had some perfect days punting on the river Cam and left the war behind for a few peaceful hours.

There seems to have been a long silence between the letters from Ben dated November 4th 1941 and March 1st 1942. It is hard to believe that we did not write to each other for Christmas that year; I probably lost the letters or they went astray in the air or on the sea.

The last letter I received from Ben in America was the one he wrote on March 1st 1942. When Ben was in California he found an article in a Magazine by E. M. Forster on the poet Crabbe, who has born in Aldeburgh and spent part of his life there. Then Ben managed to find a volume of Crabbe's poems in which was the poem *The Borough*, all about Aldeburgh. This made him more homesick than ever.

From that moment the idea of his first full-scale operas began to go round in his head and *Peter Grimes* was in embryo, although Ben's Peter was a very different character from Crabbe's. One feels that the Peter of the opera was more sinned against than sinning and cannot help feeling sorry for him, whereas Crabbe's Peter was a character with no redeeming features.

As Ben mentions in his last letter, Koussevitsky the conductor had "taken him up big", and Ben probably talked to him about the idea he had of writing an opera. In any case, Koussevitsky commissioned Ben to write the opera and gave him £100 to write it. Ben dedicated *Peter Grimes* to the memory of Koussevitsky's wife, Natalie, and it was written for the Koussevitsky Music Foundation.

March 1st 1942

c/o Dr. Mayer,
Long Island Home,
Amityville, N.Y.

My dear Kit,

Your letter arrived a few days ago, very much delayed like all the mail these days. Thank you very much for it. I am sorry I have been so bad about writing lately, but I'm afraid I can never get up much enthusiasm about letter-writing, finding that a pen for me moves more easily in crotchets than in letters; and also, these days, when things happen so quickly, & the general outlook changes so fast, that it is hopeless to write about one's life at all, knowing perfectly well that the letter will be hopelessly out of date on arrival. Anyhow, as you would imagine, my life has been, like everyone else's over here, changed somewhat by the declaration of war, & still to this moment I am not quite sure what will happen to me. I have certain things I want to do and which I may or may not be able to do – when I know I'll let you & Beth know, of course. Until this happens, one tries to go on working – luckily, I believe in my work, and so don't fall into the obvious dangers of half-heartedness, which so many artists feel like these days – but working is difficult, because there are so many distractions, endless red-tape, business matters etc, which have nothing to do & seriously interfere with the extraordinarily complicated matter of writing music. Actually, I have had a pretty good success this season, far and away better than any other – Koussevitsky has taken me up big, and I have had good successes with a string quartet, <u>Les Illuminations</u> (which Peter has sung a few times) and a show with the Philadelphia under Ormandy. Which is all gratifying. But what really worries me now is that I have reached a definite turning point in my work, & what I most want is to be able to think & think & work & work, completely undistracted for a good period of time. If it were in normal times this would be completely possible – but, my problem is only that of probably about 40,000,000 young ambitious men. I cannot tell you how much I agree with and admire your letter. I am so pleased that you have thought things out so carefully. From a very different angle I have come to an identical point-of-view (re discipline & obedience) – but in art, as you know, the bias is to the other direction, that of anarchy & romantic "freedom". A carefully chosen discipline is the only possible course. I am terribly sorry that you are having such a difficult time. It is only small comfort to think that so many others are in similar positions, and that it can't last forever.

America has been strange since the actually entry into the war. At first there was terrific excitement, "unity" (howoften have we heard that word!), and flag waving. Now most of the first two have disappeared – after all the Pacific is a mighty long way away, and bad news (vide, China, Spain, Poland, London, Coventry ad infinitum) grows boring after atime, unless you happen to have a brother or an aunt near the danger spot. Politics are filthy here, as you know, and so after the first shock, people are squabbling in the highest places as before. The flag-waving remains, because so many people like doing it, & adore wearing uniforms (without exception hideous) – but it makes me sick, especially as I loathe the Star-Spangled Banner and its awkward harmonies. There has been a certain effort to ban German & Italian music, which hasn't luckily succeeded, & apart from some ludicrous restrictions on enemy aliens (99% refugees of course – everyone knows that most of the fifth columnists are settled citizens of, maybe, German extraction,) people have kept their heads. Of course everyone is numbered, docketed, finger printed, photographed, registered – but one gets used to that. The Radio, you mentioned "news", is fantastic here of course. On the medium wave-length, there must be 100 different stations everyone can get – & from every one is blared forth the most startling news items, preceded, interrupted & concluded by the most blatant and, usually, intimate advertisements.

Newspapers, except maybe the Times, are completely unreliable. The magnates have just discovered, I gather, that good news sells best, so judging by head-lines, the Jap fleet has been sunk twice-over, Singapore was invincible until a day or so before it fell, ditto, the Phillipines, Rangoon, & I support Java et al. There is here as much Anti-British feeling as there is Anti-Yank with you. The British are stupid here – so superior, and the Gneisenau and Scharnhorst episode, Libyan news, & Singapore coming all to-gether have made so many little arm-chair strategists & "know-alls" go about saying that the British have never won a war & now are depending upon Russia & America to do the job. Churchill goes over big – especially the flowery phrases . . . . well . . . Cripps has a good press, too. But India stinks. So might their own treatment of the negroes, but that doesn't occur to them. The thing that really is bringing the war home is the rationing of tyres, & sugar (consequently Coca-Cola).

I am putting a note to Beth in this – please tell her all the news – I haven't got time to write her a long letter I'm afraid. I was delighted to hear about the yacht designing: I haven't been able to get a copy of the magazine yet, but I'm hoping too. It must have been a thrill. Have you any more coming along? [My husband designed boats.]

Please excuse writing – never my strongest point!

Yours ever, Ben.

March 1st 1942

Amityville, N.Y.

My darling Beth,

Please forgive my not writing before – well I've given Kit all the usual reasons, but honestly these last months have been unusually hectic, in every direction. I have to write so many tiresome little letters that I never have the time or energy to get round to the big ones. Anyhow – I don't think yet that I've told you what a thrill & delight Enid's pictures of you & Sebastian, & Barbara were. He really is an amazing child – where did he get his looks from? – & I think I know him well from the pictures now, they are really awfully good – of him, that's to say: you are hopeless, my dear! If I didn't know you already I should think you were a strange, bashful thing! Barbara was much more brave. But I shouldn't talk, being hopeless too in front of a camera. Anyhow – I was bucked to get them, & I show them to nearly everyone who comes to the house. It has been rotten for you to have Kit away; luckily you seem to have seen him quite a bit, and anyhow you have the kid, who must be a blessing. So sorry that things in Peasenhall don't go so well. I had a nice letter from D, & Himself too, only his was completely cut to pieces by the censor. Goodness knows what he said! [. . .]

always your   Ben.

176

21

Home from America

When Ben wrote the letter on March 1st, they were waiting for a passage home. They left on March 16th 1942. Wystan Auden was sad to see them go, although he came later, and entered the army. He and Ben were never such good friends again, although they met several times after this, Elizabeth Mayer tried to get them together but it was no good. Elizabeth remained close to Wystan, and worked together with him translating many of his works into German and other languages. Ben told me that Peter got him away from Auden.

It was good that they did not tell us that they were coming, they had to wait weeks for a passage, and finally got a berth on a Swedish cargo boat *The Axel Johnson*, they were in a convoy, the U boat menace was at its height, and when the boat's funnel caught on fire the convoy had to go on without them, and there they were a sitting target in the middle of the Atlantic. In spite of this really harrowing experience Ben managed to write the *Ceremony of Carols*, and the *Hymn to St Cecilia* cooped up in a tiny cabin next to the refrigerator.

Barbara received a telegram from Liverpool asking her if she could put Ben up for the night, she immediately telephoned me. We were overjoyed of course and I rushed into a train (we were in Northwood then) to go and see him. It was very thoughtful of them not to tell us they were coming, we should have been so worried. Of course we never stopped talking, he had been away for three years, and looked much older. They were both very shocked to see the effects of the Blitz on London.

As soon as Ben had contacted the people he wanted to see in London he went down to Snape. We had kept the Morris 8 for him, and although petrol was very short, we got about two gallons a month for shopping and urgent journeys, there was no public transport in Snape, except for a bus that went to Ipswich one Saturday and came back the next Saturday. Fortunately Ben was a great walker and we had some ancient bicycles, so he could get onto his beloved marshes.

As Ben and Peter were confirmed pacifists it was obvious that they would have to face a tribunal, on their return to this country. Ben was offered the job of the conductor of the R A F band. Many musicians had escaped fighting by joining the band. Ben refused this, he would have to wear a uniform and that he would not do. It would have been an easy way out. The first tribunal went badly for them both, we thought they would have to go to prison, as Michael Tippett had had to do. It was suggested that they should appeal, and this time it went better. In fact Ben was told to get on with his job of composing, and Peter to join the Council for Encouragement of Music and the Arts (C E M A). In fact Ben did not have to do anything except write music but he did go with Peter to give concerts round the country. Maria Korchinska the harpist often went with them, they landed up in the most peculiar places, sometimes in village halls with impossible pianos, and the audience knowing nothing about serious music.

Now Ben based himself at the Snape Mill, where he was happiest at writing, but he always had to have a place to go to in London, so in future it was Peter who found and looked after the London flats, he was getting anxious about his parents who were getting old and needed looking after, and then some good friends of theirs Erwin and Sophie Stein and their young daughter Marion, were burnt out of their flat, and a larger place became necessary. They took in the Steins, and Peter started on a disastrous course of buying large houses to house all these people. Somehow they never seemed quite right. The one in Bayswater was a real white elephant, a typical narrow London house with a basement kitchen, where poor Sophie Stein had to cook for that motley group.

The Old Mill began filling up with guests as Ben began on the composing of *Peter Grimes*. He found a variety of people from the village to do things in the house and garden. I was at that time in Buxton where Kit had been sent by the R A F, I was becoming fed up with furnished houses, and there was another baby on the way, it was difficult being a camp follower with one child, but with two it would be worse. I wrote to Ben and very sweetly he said that I could come to the Mill for as long as I liked, which considering it now was a generous thing to do, to invite a pregnant woman and a small boy of three into his home. I arrived before Christmas, and the baby, Sally was born on January 13th 1943.

One of the many people who stayed with us was Edward Sackville-West, who was extremely kind to me, and taught me how to make a sauce, and helped me in the kitchen. He told us about his home in Kent, Knole. The roof was so large that seven men were permanently employed to look after it. Rather a different affair from the old Mill and the tiny kitchen there, Ben was collaborating with Eddie on a melodrama for broadcasting entitled *The Rescue*. With all this in hand at the beginning of March 1943, he was struck down with measles and carried off to the Grove fever hospital in Tooting.

*

Ben wrote to me at the Mill:

Sunday

Many thanks for your sweet letter. Yes, isn't this just crazy! I don't mind so much now that I feel better (I felt pretty low for about a week), but it is awfully boring sitting here in one place when there are so many things that I want to do! No visitors are allowed, but I believe that Barbara (& possibly Peter) are being given special permission to visit me today. I am being treated very condescendingly – I was in a ward with 2 others (kids) for 2 days, but I have a room to myself since & a fire, & a doctor has lent me magazines, & Enid sent me some good books – so I can't complain! I don't know how long I shall have to stay here (probably only about 10 days more), then I hope to come down to Snape for a nice long convalescence – if you'll have me!

The garden sounds very exciting. Has the gardener turned up & is he efficient? I owe you lots of money for all these things – but I hope you don't mind waiting for a bit because I haven't got my cheque book here!

I am glad Sebastian takes such an interest in the garden as to use his phlumpth pot! Sorry Sally's getting like me – can't you give her a face massage, or something to stop it? How I'm longing to see you all again. Enid's photos are wonderful – especially the one of you bringing up Sally's wind. She has a wonderful look of concentration! If there is anything I want, Barbara will call & ask you. I'm not sure yet what I can have – but I should imagine honey would be allowed & I should adore some. The food is pretty dismal. All very LCC.

What news of Kit? Give him my love when you write.

No more now my dear – write again soon

Love to the lot of you.

Ben.

The "Enid" Ben writes about in his letter was Montagu Slater's wife. Montagu was writing the libretto for *Peter Grimes*. The Slater family became frequent visitors at the Mill, usually bringing their youngest daughter Carol with them. Enid was a professional photographer and she took some wonderful pictures of the children.

"Phlumpth" was the word Sebastian had given to going on his pot. He was always a great one for inventing words. He gave names to all and sundry. His paternal grandmother he called "Cuckoo", because when she saw him coming in his pram as a baby she waved to him and called "Cuckoo!" The name stuck to her all through her life, much to her annoyance. Everyone including her sons always called her that. "Beisha" was his name for his grand-father, which also stuck with all the family. No one knew how that came about. Sebastian called the cat "Blatelus", and when that one departed the next cat was Susie Blatelus.

March 10th 1943

Grove Hospital,
Tooting Grove,
SW 17

My darling old Beth,

What a <u>lovely</u> parcel! It really is just like being back at School again – the excitement of having addition to the terribly dull menu – & a cake too. I have written a note to Mrs Burrows – I thought she'd like it. But it is sweet of you my dear to take the trouble, I know how busy you are – but if you knew how I love the eggs for breakfast & what a difference the cake makes to the incredibly dull teas, you'd feel rewarded!

I am getting on slowly. It is pretty dull, but I've been provided with lots of books (Peter brought some, Enid [Slater] sent two, & Clifford [Curzon] one excellent batch), & the doctors come & talk quite abit, so it might be worse. I wish the old German planes would let us alone, tho'. I hate it in here – Not bad but just irritating, but what these poor South Londoners suffer I'm getting an inkling of now. [. . .]

How's Snape & Sally & Sebastian & Suzie Blattelas & all? Gosh, how I'm longing to come down to you all. I should be out on Tuesday next week, & down to you on the Wednesday or Thursday I should think? It will be heaven, but I hope not too much trouble for you, my dear.

I am getting some pretty strong opinions on the nursing profession. Of course they're terribly overworked here, & I shouldn't think one gets the best types at Tooting! – but, all the same . . . . . I'll tell you when I see you.

Much love my dear, take care of yourself, & many many thanks,
Love   Ben
Love to Kit when you write or call him.

Ben came to the Mill as soon as he could get away from the hospital, looking very pale. He had had a rough time, but was feeling very proud of himself, as he had given blood for the adult serum needed to save the lives of babies under a year who contracted measles, whereas none of the other men in the hospital had agreed to do so although among them were big strong navvies. When Ben got into his own bed again, he smoothed the sheets and remarked gratefully how smooth they were compared with the hospital sheets. He soon recovered and started work again.

Some time after this Ben had a bad patch. He lost his creative powers and was convinced he would never write anything again, thinking of all the composers he had heard of who had dried up when young. It seemed to be a long time, but actually it was probably only two or three weeks. He spent the time walking across the marshes, walking in fact anywhere, everywhere, I did my best to comfort and encourage him; we were in despair. At last it came back.

We had to think which was the safest place in the Mill to be when there were air raids. Ben's studio in the Mill itself seemed to be the best place. The Mill-post in the centre of the studio had stood up to the weight and strain of the great sails turning in the wind. If we received a direct hit there was nothing we could do except protect ourselves from flying glass, so we blocked the windows with furniture as best we could. We took mattresses into the studio so that we could be ready to go there at any moment. We had to keep the bedding away from the drips that came in a circle on the side of the studio where the balcony joined the bedroom above. Ever since the Mill roof had been raised to make a bedroom for Ben, and the balcony made outside the bedroom window, there had been drips. The drips came through the ceiling into the studio in a semi-circle, just missing Ben's working table. The balcony floor was covered with lead and it should have been watertight but it was not. I am told by the present owner that the problem is still with them, although they have hopes of curing it. We had to put anything we could find to catch the drips, they were all metal, there was no plastic then, so there was a concert of "ping-pong-ping-pong-pang", during heavy rain. It is a wonder that these sounds did not enter the music that Ben was writing at the time.

One evening when Ben was frantically trying to finish a piece, it was raining heavily, and the usual buckets had been put in place. He came to me in despair. "Can't something be done to stop these drips?" he wailed. Not at the time being able to think of anything else to do, we went up into his bedroom and tore down the wall under the window to see if we could find out where the water was coming in. We traced the trickle of water quite a long way, then at last lost it.

Maybe when Benjamin came to write his first Church Parable *Noyes Fludde* the memory of the drips he had to put up with at the Mill, came back to him. He finally achieved the sound of rain drops by hanging on string at intervals a series of china mugs, which were tapped with a wooden spoon.

When the air-raids were persistent we spent many nights sleeping on the Mill floor; the bedding had to be placed so as to avoid the trickle of water running across the floor, for sometimes the drips changed direction and missed the buckets. We put the children's beds under the piano, thinking that was the safest place for them to be. The night the farm in Priory Lane received a direct hit from a V-1 (one of the flying-bombs or "doodle-bugs" as they were mostly called), we were all in the Mill. Sally, aged two, woke up and said "Bang!" Sebastian did not stir, although it was a terrific noise, the farm being only half a mile away. The explosion brought down the ceiling in the sittingroom and broke many of the windows in the building.

We could watch the doodlebugs as they were passing over Thorpeness, and trace the direction in which they were flying by their tail lights. If they turned and went down the coast towards Ipswich, we were safe, but if they turned inland they came in our direction and we needed to take cover. When Ben was at home we took turns to go outside and see which way they were going. One night Ben had gone outside to look. Suddenly there was a great clatter and I thought "This is IT!" Actually, Ben had fallen over a pile of toys which the children had left in the porch, in his hurry to come back and tell me the flying bomb had headed down the coast.

Ben was so good and patient about the noise and mess the children made. The radio was in our sitting-room/dining-room, so that if he wanted to listen to something and we were all there having a meal, he would crouch down with his ear to the loudspeaker remarking that it was as well his concentration was so good. Of course the children were not allowed in the Studio and, when he was working, I tried to keep them away from the Studio windows. We often had other children with us: our nephew Alan Britten and Carol Slater, who came with her parents when

Montagu was working on the *Peter Grimes* script with Ben. Enid brought her camera and took some marvellous pictures of us and the marshes.

Many people have the idea that musicians, artists and writers work by inspiration, frantically working while the inspiration lasts. That was not the way Benjamin worked. When he was working at home, he kept regular hours and wrote to a set pattern. Always an early riser he would be in his studio at least by 9.0 a.m., working through until 1.0 o'clock with a break for coffee, then a light lunch and some form of exercise. In the summer, after the war, he played tennis or cricket if the people and the place were available. Otherwise he walked, either by himself or with a friend or relation, who had to be in training, for he walked far and fast. He did much of the planning for future compositions on these walks and sometimes sang as he went. One day he came back from one of these walks laughing. He had been walking along the road past the Maltings, singing at the top of his voice and waving his stick in the air, when he suddenly realised that a group of people were staring at him. "They must have thought I was mad," he said.

Sometimes, when I went to take him his coffee, I found Ben reading a "who-dunnit". When I looked surprised, he would look up guiltily and say that it relaxed him. After the afternoon walk and a cup of tea, Ben returned to his studio and worked again solidly for three more hours; then dinner, perhaps a read or a game, and bed. This was the pattern he followed throughout his life, when he was able to be at home, in Snape and later on in Aldeburgh.

He was always happiest when he could be in his beloved Suffolk, writing music and seeing friends. People in London complained that he shut himself away, but I am sure that is what he had to do when he could possibly manage it. He had to be away a great deal for rehearsals, performances and meetings, and this increased tremendously after the war, and after his opera *Peter Grimes* took the country by storm. Very often Peter and Ben would drive back home to Suffolk in the middle of the night so as not to lose a moment there.

[Undated, probably August 1944]

Old Mill.

My dear old thing,

Your letter came this morning (Monday) – but I expect that by now you will have received Barbara's telling you about this weekend. We have had a nice time; Christina & Mrs Burrows looked after us well & we've been well fed too. Spent most of the time sleeping – making up for last week, which was pretty hectic. I go back with Barbara this afternoon – have to go to the Behrends on Thursday until Monday, & then down here – Unless I have to go down to Dartington to help Cicely cope as Chris died suddenly yesterday. It's very sad as he was getting on so well, & I just had a very hopeful letter. But I don't think it'll be necessary for me to go, & I'd much rather come to Snape.

I'm so glad that you're having a good time – hope Sebastian's better. Love to everyone. I hope the journey back will go as well as the one their [sic]. By-the-way, the jumper [the old Morris 8] <u>may</u> be at Wesby's if he hasn't been able to bring it back – we've got to go in it this afternoon because we can't get a taxi. So if you want it you 'd better 'phone him.

Love Ben

I've paid Mrs Burrows & Christina but not Hart (a) because I didn't see him (b) because I didn't know how much you'd fixed with him.

We've looked after the tomatos like delicate children – they're doing fine!

22

Peter Grimes and the Chamber Operas

The bombings were easing up as the war in Europe was drawing to a close, and towards the end of the year Ben at last finished writing *Peter Grimes.* He had had trouble getting Montagu Slater to write the libretto as he wanted it. Although he was happy with most of what Montagu wrote, some parts of it he literally wrote himself. The best librettist may be someone who does not object to having his work altered.

Now came the anxious business of the production. The part of Peter Grimes was written specially for Peter Pears and Ben wanted Joan Cross to sing the part of Ellen Orford. He had heard her sing often with the Sadler's Wells Opera Company and felt that she was just the person he wanted to play the part. Joan had often been to stay with us at the Mill and she had helped Ben a lot by singing some of the songs with him. With her experience of opera production – she had been Director of the Sadler's Wells Opera Company since 1941 – throughout the difficult times during the war when they had no permanent home, Sadler's Wells being shut for the duration, she could give Ben much good advice.

Kenneth Green was asked to design the sets. He was then art master at Wellington College and had been a friend for some years. The Green family had lived for some time in Southwold, so Kenneth also had roots in Suffolk. Eric Crozier was asked to produce the opera, but where was it to be performed? Ralph Hawkes, Ben's publisher, wanted the first performance to be at Covent Garden, as Boosey and Hawkes were closely involved in a plan to reopen the Royal Opera House as a National Opera and had it in mind to present Ben's new opera. But Tyrone Guthrie, Lawrence Collingwood and Joan Cross, the administrators of Sadler's Wells, which was also to be reopened, had heard Ben play through *Peter Grimes* on the piano, and they also wanted to open the Wells with this entirely new form of English opera. After much discussion, it was agreed the opera should open Sadler's Wells.

What was not taken into consideration, however, was how the company would react to this. They were at the end of four years of hard touring, putting up with wartime privations, having to rehearse in unsuitable and difficult conditions. So when the rumour of a return to Sadler's Wells trickled through, they thought they would be back to where it all stopped in 1939. One or two of the first class voices had spent wasteful years singing parts that had in no way extended them. They therefore hoped for a return to singing star roles in their favourite operas Instead of this, they were offered parts in a new opera with a very strange story and in a musical idiom difficult and alien to them.

As Joan Cross told me: "It seems almost impossible nowadays to try to accept their attitude": a letter from one of the musical staff at the time wrote of the "sheer strain imposed on all the voices" – the lynching chorus in Act III is really a killer, especially when you consider the size of the chorus – thirty-two. This was forty years ago and choruses have become accustomed to singing far more complicated assignments since. Resentments grew. Even though the long cast of *Grimes* absorbed most of the personnel, there had to be some omissions and those left out felt that they had been slighted. Benjamin adamantly refused the performance unless Joan sang the part of Ellen, which put her into an embarrassing position. Her job was in management and there were other sopranos who thought they should have been asked to sing the leading female role. Finally, Joan agreed to sing the part of Ellen and resigned from management. Tony Guthrie therefore undertook to run the company and became involved in many meetings which were both acrimonious and time-consuming.

Joan had a miserable time. There were rumours, quite unfounded, that she was proposing to turn Sadler's Wells into an opera school and that the Royal Opera House would take over the existing resources. Tony Guthrie told the company that their standard was so low that they would be lucky if Covent Garden would take them on as an entity, which did not help at all. Joan took part in the arguments, but she was very grieved that all the efforts of the war period, when they had some good successes, had ended so sadly.

So it was that rehearsals started with little enthusiasm from the singers and the orchestra. However on reaching the first Sea Interlude, they were bowled over. Joan says that she was knocked sideways by the beauty of the music, in spite of that the atmosphere was still unpleasant, but the fact that the first performance survived aggravating and unhappy circumstances is operatic history. *Grimes* has easily survived and that small, exhausted, confused group of singers are on record for their part in the world première. No one could imagine how the piece would be received, but on the first night Tony Guthrie was heard to say: "Whatever happens we were right to do it."

In fact, the new opera was an immediate success: "the music is fascinating", "has force, vitality, beauty", "full of power and emotional intensity" – "Britten took an ovation from an audience containing some of the greatest names in music" – "one of the most exciting events for years" – "the only grand opera chorus which ever acted" – these were among some of the notices the first performance received.

Those first performances unfortunately were never recorded. Decca offered to record the piece, but the company, still largely hostile, voted against this in favour of entertaining the army with an ENSA tour in Germany. No doubt a commendable decision, but it robbed posterity of any record of those first performances.

While all this was going on in London, my younger daughter, Elizabeth Rosemary Ellen (Ellen, after Ellen Orford), was born at the Old Mill, Snape, on April 21st, 1945. For this reason, I was not able to go to the first performance of *Peter Grimes* on June 7th – a great sadness to me. I could not leave the baby, she was very small and when she was born it took a few weeks to get her really strong.

As Arthur Oldham writes in the book *Benjamin Britten, a Commentary on his works* (edited by Donald Mitchell and Hans Keller, 1952):

> The impact on the musical world of the first performance of *Peter Grimes* on 7th June, 1945 ... was immense. At first the reaction was astonishment. Later it changed to delight mingled with apprehension ... The majority of people before that night would not have believed it possible that an English composer was about to make a contribution to operatic literature which would not only be on a level equal to the highest contemporary musical standards, but become a major box office attraction in the repertory theatres throughout the world. Since the death of Purcell, many English composers had attempted to do the same thing; all, to a greater or lesser degree, had failed. We had suffered the discomfort of seeing our literary classics become operatic masterpieces in the hands of an Italian genius and had been powerless to compete. By 1945, the failure of English opera had become axiomatic. It seemed too good to be true that, after two hundred years of disillusionment, England was again to lead the world in this most complicated sphere of musical achievement.

I remember well the tremendous success the opera achieved. Even the Daily Mail had a huge write-up on its front page, and this was not a newspaper that normally took interest in classical music. It seemed as though Ben had hit the right moment for his new work, just a few weeks after the end of the war in Europe, when everyone was thankful, but tired and disillusioned in spite of winning the war. Here was something tremendous, other than guns and victory in war, produced by an Englishman. Ben had vindicated the wise tribunal that let him get on with his composing, rather than sending him to prison or to work on a farm.

Ben was not one to rest on his laurels, for he had already started work on the next opera *The Rape of Lucretia.* The difficulties he had experienced with a large chorus and orchestra in the production of *Grimes* made him think seriously before starting on another large scale opera. He thought also that there would be problems in the post-war world for the production of opera. Therefore he decided to try another form altogether, chamber opera. This would require a small chamber orchestra, with the minimum number of singers and no chorus, and it would therefore be much cheaper to produce.

Ronald Duncan was asked to write the libretto and it was decided to use André Obey's recent realisation of the Lucretia legend, which uses two narrators, the Male and Female Chorus, to be sung by Peter Pears and Joan Cross. Joan was to sing all the important roles in Ben's operas until she retired after singing the part of the Housekeeper in *The Turn of the Screw.*

At Snape we had a new lot of people to stay with us, including Ronald and Rose Marie Duncan and sometimes their two children, Bryony and Roger, for instance. When all four of them were together it was the most extraordinary contrast. Ronnie was very dark and small-boned, Rose Marie very blond; whereas Bryony was like Rose Marie, very fair, and Roger very dark, like Ronnie. I liked having Rose Marie to stay and Ben got on well with her too, not so well with Ronnie with whom he had some trouble getting the libretto the way he wanted it. In fact, after the libretto was published Ben was so dissatisfied with some parts that he had numerous alterations made in the text, which meant rewriting much of the score.

Barbara and I went to the first performance of *Lucretia* at Glyndebourne. Our little car was very shabby and was not the kind of car in which most people went to Glyndebourne. However, we drove boldly up to the stage door of the opera house and asked for Benjamin Britten – he had told us to be sure and ask for him when we arrived. The porter at the door had never heard of him. "But", we said, "he is the composer of the opera which is being performed tonight." Still no good. At last we said, "Well, take us to Mrs. Christie, please." Which he finally unwillingly did. Mrs. Christie could not have been more welcoming and kind. It was a very hot day, and we were hot and tired after the drive from London, and she gave us the most delicious iced tea I have ever tasted. Soon Ben was there and the rest of the cast, including Kathleen Ferrier, who was to sing Lucretia, having finally been persuaded by Ben to undertake the part. She had never sung in opera before and was nervous and unsure of her acting ability.

I shall never forget that first performance. It is sad that *The Rape of Lucretia* is less popular than the other chamber operas and is less often performed, because I think it has some of the most beautiful music Benjamin ever wrote. *The Ride to Rome,* sung by Peter at Glyndebourne, was so exciting I found I was clutching my dress with sweaty hands. One could almost see Tarquinius crossing the Tiber; and Lucretia's final entrance – Kathleen walking slowly onto the stage in a purple dress – took one's breath away with its pathos.

It was a strange thing about Kathleen. When I first knew her, she was always lovable and funny and dear, but I never thought her beautiful then. As time went on she literally grew beautiful. What a terrible loss was her early death, not only to music but to everyone with whom she came in contact. Ben loved her dearly and was so sad that nothing is recorded of her singing his songs. Aunt Flo tried her hardest to understand Ben's music, but being so utterly unmusical it was a struggle. She said the singers screeched. Once, when she was staying with my husband and me, I took her to dinner with Ben at Crag House in Aldeburgh and then to a performance of *The Rape of Lucretia* in the Jubilee Hall, on Saturday June 12th, 1954. At the end of Scene 2, Act I, Aunt Flo whispered to me: "Why can't Benjamin let the maids go to bed, and not keep them up so late?" Afterwards, however, she said she had enjoyed most of it.

A propos of *Lucretia,* when Queen Mary attended a performance of the opera at Glyndebourne, Benjamin was introduced to her at the end and she asked him: "Tell me, Mr. Britten, what made you choose such a subject?" Rather taken aback, Ben answered, "Well, I am rather interested in that sort of thing." Somebody overheard Ben say this and, of course, soon everyone had heard of it. It took him a long time to live that down.

While *Lucretia* was still in production, *Albert Herring* was already on the way. Eric Crozier this time was to be librettist, and it was to be quite different from the first two operas; a chamber opera, but a comic one, based on a short story by Guy de Maupassant, *Le Rosier de Madame Husson.*

Ben thoroughly enjoyed working on this and he really let himself go in the brilliant characterisation of the roles. He modelled Lady Billows on my mother-in-law, with exaggeration of course, but Cuckoo liked to think herself the Queen Bee of the village and was a terrible snob. Ben threatened to call the schoolmistress Miss Welford, but I dissuaded him and he called her Miss Wordsworth instead.

23

Goodbye to the Old Mill

At this time we had been living at the Old Mill, but Kit and I had for some while been house-hunting in the Woodbridge area. We had bought a practice in the village of Otley and Kit had been commuting from Snape to Otley, which became impossible for him, especially for night calls. Finally we had to be content with a very large run-down house near Woodbridge, which had been occupied by the army. We spent the first years taking coal out of the cupboards in the house and throwing away tins which occupied most of the garden. So rather sadly I had to leave Ben and Snape in September 1946 and our life together came to an end. Ben and Peter did not stay on much longer in Snape. Ben longed for the sea and in 1947 they moved to Aldeburgh to Crag House, Crabbe Street.

After we left the Old Mill, I was to continue to see Ben at fairly frequent intervals After the enormous success of *Peter Grimes,* his name was finally made as an important composer. At last perhaps here was the re-birth of English opera, and he was in demand everywhere. Operas and other works came from him thick and fast: After *Grimes, Lucretia,* 1946 and *Albert Herring,* 1947, both produced at Glyndebourne; the start of the English Opera Group; the opening of the Aldeburgh Festival 1948; the cantata *St. Nicolas,* 1948; *The Beggar's Opera,* by 1948; *The Little Sweep (Let's Make an Opera),* 1949. *Billy Budd,* 1951 (for the Festival of Britain); and so on, apart from all song settings he was writing, touring with the English Opera Group and giving concerts everywhere with Peter Pears. On the occasions when I was called on to go to lunch and for walks with him, he often said "If *only* I had time to go back over the past work and correct or alter as I want to do, but always people are waiting to rehearse, and it is not fair to keep them waiting."

It was wonderful of him to find time for his family, but I think he needed us, certainly his two sisters for as the people fell round him (and I fear they often did – he had to be ruthless), we were always there, as was Peter also. He could be cross and critical of us, though he rarely was. Barbara suffered a lot when she was hostess for him during the Aldeburgh Festival. She was his whipping boy and he would fly out at her when he felt he needed to be nasty to someone. She could not take it as perhaps I could have done, and her frantic face was very much in evidence as the Festival wore on each year. I never envied her her job. I preferred to remain outside, away from the Red House, and to be able to enjoy the music.

People are always asking: "Aren't you proud of your famous brother?" I was, of course, but often wished he was not so famous so that one could see more of this brother who was such a joy to be with. Janet Baker has written that the air crackled when he walked into the room, and she was right. He was so wise and always had sympathy with one's worries and troubles; he always found time to listen.

When fame started to come to Benjamin, he enjoyed it – Barbara and I used to chaff him when we thought he took too many curtain calls – but as time went on fame became a burden. This was one of the reasons he and Peter had to leave Crag House. Passers-by would peer over the fence and, when they made the fence higher, peered through the holes. There was no privacy. The move was a great sadness, for Ben could no longer work looking out at his beloved sea. He told me that one of the worst things was to be travelling in a train and to hear someone start talking about him, without recognising him. "What do you do then?" I asked. He said: "I go outside and stand in the corridor, or move into another carriage."

While they were still living at Crag House, the Music Club of Aldeburgh was inaugurated. In 1950 John Stevens, who was a chemist, and his wife Thelma, were looking for a business to buy. A chemist's shop came up for sale in Aldeburgh and, as they were both very musical, they decided to come there, for they felt sure there would be plenty of musical activities for them in a place where there was the Aldeburgh Festival and where Benjamin Britten and Peter Pears were living.

They found there was in fact very little music going on, apart from the Festival, and in those early days that lasted for only ten days in June. John Stevens remarked to Ben one day that they were disappointed that there was so little music in the town. Ben said it was a pity and what did John suggest? John said, could they not start a club? He knew there were plenty of musical people around. Ben asked him to make a list and said he would call a meeting at Crag House. The meeting was arranged and there was much enthusiasm for the idea, so on April 8th 1952 the first Committee Meeting of the Aldeburgh Music Club was held in Crag House. It was decided that the membership should be open to all practising musicians in Aldeburgh and district, amateur or professional, with a subscription of five shillings a year for incidental expenses. The following announcement was circulated:

The first meeting will be held on Sunday, May 11th, at 8 pm at Crag House, 4 Crabbe Street, and we invite you to come and listen with a view of taking part in some future programmes.

Signed: B. Pritchard, Lillian Basham, John Stevens.

RSVP to Julia Keys, The Old Customs House, Aldeburgh.

Ben did not play the piano at these Music Club evenings, nor did Peter sing, which was tactful of them. Ben played the viola and Peter played either the recorder or the piano. The Club minutes note that after the music "Mr. Peter Pears spoke to the members about the hopes and aims of the Club, and this was followed with coffee and an informal discussion with members wishing to take part in future programmes".

The next meeting took place on May 23rd 1952, and here it is noted that "a letter was sent to Benjamin Britten and Peter Pears asking them to repeat their grand performance with another string trio, with Miss Backhouse".

The committee meetings generally were held at "Herons" (Miss Backhouse's home), whereas the music evenings were at Crag House whenever Ben or Peter were there and later at the Red House. Peter lent music from his library to the Club. Ben and Peter continued to play with them as often as possible, although as time went on their lives became more complicated and the Festival grew and grew, taking up more and more of their time, so that they were not able to go as often as before.

The Club went on from strength to strength and now it is a large affair, with a choir, a group of recorders and another of strings.

My old friend, Miss Biddy Row, when aged 92 and living alone since her sister Lorna had died, told me that she and her sister joined the Music Club very soon after its formation in 1952. She related an amusing incident. Part of the string section of the Club were to give a recital in Aldeburgh Church. The instrumentalists were Miss Rhoda Backhouse, violin (she was a very good player, really professional, and owned a Stradivarius), Biddy Row (second violin), Lorna Row (cello), Benjamin Britten (viola). They were rehearsing for the concert at Ben's house. Biddy was tapping with her foot to help her keep time. Rhoda said: "Don't do that, Biddy, it is very bad taste and common." Ben gave Biddy a sweet smile and said: "Well, I like it, it helps me to keep in time too, and please wear white shoes on Sunday in church, so that I can see them."

On a later occasion, the cellist Billy Barry was rehearsing a quartet at the Red House and wrote the following poem:

Our Schubert Quartet

The summer came, the warning knell
Run Biddy run! The telephone bell.
Tonight at 8.15, we meet . . . . .
Now don't be early, far better be late,
Than give dear Ben no time to eat
his dinner, and as you know I hate
the phone like hell, so you may ring
the Barry woman and fix up everything.

Amiable as ever Biddy hastens to obey
And everything's soon settled for the great
      auspicious day.
We arrive!
We creep into the house
Rhoda is with us, stalks on ahead
While we with manners nice
And quiet as little mice
Stay behind and quickly shed
Our outer garments – the Cello's bag;
Then in single file – on carpet red
Hurry along, no time to lag
Down the long corridor we tread.

Our leader, ready in her place
Has just time for the embrace.
And grudgingly sees Ben all smiles
Implant a kiss on Biddy's cheek
Which she accepts quite good and meek.

We take our place and Biddy starts
(Much too slow, or much too fast!!)
Rhoda looks haggard, dour and grim.

While kind Ben Britten, it seems to him
The greatest fun in the world to play
With the likes of us – in our humble way.
He never finds fault, but will often suggest
How a passage should go, or point out a rest.

Isn't it ghastly?! says Rhoda at last
And Biddy with complex so lowly and humble,
Is sure the complaint at her must be cast
And takes all the blame for this tiresome grumble.
That impossible Billy just winks at her friend
And Ben is still happy and cheering us on
With a "Wasn't so bad! Let's do it again."
Hush! There once was a bar which he really played wrong
And Biddy remarked: "It's the very last straw –
If you get out, I shan't play any more!!"

Ten o'clock, the time has come,
When Betty arrives to take us home.
No time for relaxation
(we must be there on approbation)
However thirsty, no time to drink
We're hustled out – no time to think
A stand is seized and folded wrong
Which really hinders us getting along

'Cello case held upside down
Only makes the owner frown
And Billy Barry – obstinate cuss
Refuses to hurry, refuses to fuss
And just as slow as she can be
Says calmly "better leave it to me."

Next day
In High Street, Rhoda and Biddy meet.
The wind was cold, the street was wet.

"Wasn't it ghastly?" Was all she could say.
"But of course it's terribly hard to play,
And I hope you're grateful, for being allowed
to play with 'Big Ben' you ought to be proud."

"Indeed I am grateful to him and to you
And if the street was not wet
Upon my knees I would get
To pay you the homage, I feel is your due."

As many people have written, and will write about Ben and his music, I decided to stop at this point. My story is of the Britten family and Ben's youth.

Epilogue

While Ben was writing his last opera *Death in Venice* in 1972/3, with the libretto by Myfanwy Piper, based on the story by Thomas Mann, he was becoming increasingly ill with heart problems. It was a miracle that he was able to finish – only by superhuman will-power was he able to go on to the end. He would not listen to the doctors who warned him that he must stop and undergo tests to find out what should be done.

Alas, if only he had agreed to this, he might still be with us. But by the time he arrived in the operating theatre in May 1973, his heart was in such a bad state that the operation was not successful and he was left very weak. He suffered an embolism shortly after the operation, which left him partially paralysed on the right side. He was so weakened that he was not able to go to the first performances of his opera *Death in Venice* during the 1973 Aldeburgh Festival, but a special performance was put on for him in September.

Soon after this, the opera was due to be performed in Venice. Ben was not well enough to go, which was a terrible disappointment for him. He loved Venice so much and had desperately wanted to be there for the performance.

Ben asked me if I would go and be with him at his retreat in North Suffolk, while Peter had to be in Venice for the opera. I was very glad to be able to go and care for him during this time.

I did my best to cheer him up. Each afternoon, after he had had a rest, we went for drives in the country and sometimes to the sea which he loved so much; visiting the local churches and, when he felt strong enough, going for little walks down quiet country lanes and footpaths. It was incredible how he found the way to these places – he knew Suffolk better than anyone.

As a result of the paralysis of his right side, Ben was unable to play the piano with his right hand, although he tried persistently. Friends came to play with him: Monica Venn brought her violin, and Pat Nicholson her 'cello; but it was only agony for him and had to give it up. One day he said to me: "Of all the things I cannot do now, the thing I mind about the most is not being able to play the piano. My piano (in the library at the Red House) looks at me accusingly".

We waited anxiously for a word from Venice to let us know how the opera had gone and how it had been received: Nothing came. Then I received a message from the Red House that William Plomer had died. How was I going to break the news to Ben? He was so fond of William and would feel his loss deeply. Poor old boy, he was very upset, he cried; he was so weak. Laurens and Ingaret van der Post, also close friends of William's, were a great comfort at this time. I was frantic how to take his mind off Venice and William. Suddenly I had an inspiration – the letters of my father's that had recently come to light! So I fetched them from home and gave them to him to read. He really loved reading them and was so happy that Pop spoke so sweetly and so proudly of him. He was a bit annoyed with me that I had not got them in order. Never mind, thought I, it is better that he should be so! He was not really cross, but his mind was so meticulous and mine was always so muddle-headed – I could never get things in order.

Still no word from Venice. But I heard the news that Kit (my ex-husband) had died, and this time it was Ben who comforted me. At last the interminable ten days were past but there was still no news from Venice. I drove him back to the Red House, to find a telegram waiting there. Ben asked: "When did this come?" "Oh, it came a few days ago, but as it was in a foreign language we didn't know what to do!! The other news that awaited us was the death of Wystan Auden. Three deaths in so short a time; I think Ben felt that he would probably be next. However, the crowd eventually came back from Venice, full of the great success that *Death in Venice* had had there.

Throughout the winter of 1973–4 I went with Ben to his retreat in Horham, mostly when Peter Pears had to be away: He needed one or the other of us. It was marvellous to be with him again, although it nearly broke one's heart to see how weak he was and how he struggled to do everything he possibly could.

A major problem for him was that he lost his creative powers for some time, although he never gave up trying to write, and searched among some early unpublished works to rearrange them and so keep in practice. Then, marvellously, his powers returned and I hoped, how I hoped, that his health would return, especially when his hair began to grow curly again. Alas, his body remained as weak as ever, and he found writing with the stricken right hand very hard. After his sixtieth birthday, however, he managed to write a word or two to everyone who had sent greetings, and there were hundreds.

This incredibly brave, kind man – world-famous but never too grand to consider others or lend a helping hand – he always would try to come and help with the washing-up or any menial chore that one was doing. But that was typical of his consideration for others, especially for the people who worked for him. A retired matron, Susie Walton, who looked after Ben while Rita Thomson, his regular nurse, was away, told me with tears in her eyes that one afternoon, shortly before Ben died, she was getting ready to go home and went to say goodbye to him. "Have you got something for your supper, Susie?" he asked. She was overcome that he should think of that, when he was feeling so ill and suffering all the time from nausea. She told me that she considered it a great privilege to have been able to look after Benjamin. During the last weeks, Susie was looking after him at night while Rita Thomson looked after him during the day. She said she was nearly on her knees, but she refused to give up. This was marvellous of her, as she had been retired for some time, and constant night duty at her age was not funny; but she said she could not bear to think of him having a stranger care for him.

When Ben's regular doctor, Dr. Ian Tait, was away, Dr. John Stevens took charge and he would let me go and talk to him whenever I needed comfort: he was full of admiration for Ben. He had wanted him to have heroin or another drug to give him relief, but Ben absolutely refused to take anything which he thought might affect his mind. He wished to remain completely clear and conscious to the end, however uncomfortable he felt. No one could have been looked after with more devotion and loving care than he was.

Whenever possible, Ben struggled to go to the Maltings Concert Hall if there was a performance, although it was agonising for him to be there and to be unable to take part in anything. The audience would glance anxiously at the box to see if Ben was there and they were delighted if he was.

For three weeks before Ben died, we thought that every day must be the last. Rosamund Strode, his devoted musical assistant, said, "I feel sure he'll live up to Purcell's death date". Ben had a great affinity with Purcell. Rosamund also told me that when Ben was writing *Death in Venice* it was like having a wolf behind her, for she could scarcely keep ahead of him, such was his haste to get it finished!

But on one of the last occasions I saw Ben it was actually about two weeks before his death. As I was standing in his bedroom, he said to me, "If this is it, and I am sure it is, I want to go. I can't bear to go on any longer not being able to do all the things I used to do."

I remember that it was raining, and as I looked out of his bedroom window at the falling leaves on the cherry tree, I could hardly speak. However, I replied, "We can't do without you."

He answered, "You have got to." Then, when I left him, he said to me, "If ever you need help, talk to Leslie Brown. He will help you as he's helped me more than I can say." Leslie was then the Bishop of Ipswich and St. Edmundsbury. Ben had not been a regular churchgoer during the main part of his adult life. Although we were brought up by our mother to go to church regularly, he obviously felt the need for some kind of worship and had been through many different phases. At one time he nearly became a Quaker as he always had a tremendous admiration for them. At another time, the Roman Catholic church attracted him: I think he felt that their religion seemed more alive than did our Church of England; and he considered their music better. Yet in spite of all these searchings, Ben finally returned to his mother's church (the Church of England) at the end of his life. The Bishop, like nearly everyone who knew Ben, grew to love and admire him.

In the address which the Bishop gave at Ben's funeral, he said:

> "I do not believe that Ben could be dishonest. He believed deeply in a Reality which works in us and through us and is the source of goodness and beauty, joy and love. He was sometimes troubled because he was not sure if he could give the name of God to that Reality.
>
> Sometimes he looked back nostalgically to the clear, untroubled faith in Christ he had had as a boy. He was scrupulously honest about his faith, and he wrestled at a deep level with doubt and depression. I was moved to hear Dr Malcolm Williamson's report of a conversation with Ben in his box at the Maltings. Malcolm Williamson had said he felt he was in a tunnel and Ben had replied: 'There is light at the end of the tunnel'. Ben found that light. I believe he now walks in that light."

The Bishop concluded his address:

> "Ben will like the sound of the trumpets, though he will find it difficult to believe they are sounding for him."

And so, I will say Goodbye, my Ben, repeating the words my father wrote when he died: "It's grand to have known you and have your love."   Beth.

Appendix

Thomas Britten

Birkenhead street directories 1865–68.

    54 Argyle Street – Ginders and Britten silk mercers and drapers 1870 Birkenhead Trades directory;

    Britten, Thomas, silk mercer and general draper 54 Argyle Street 1866 and 1868 Electoral Registers show Thomas Britten, place of abode as St Joseph's Road, Holt Hill, although at that time his qualification for a vote was by virtue of his house at 54 Argyle Street. It was only in the 1870 Electoral Register that Thomas Britten was shown as living at 54 Argyle Street.

Name	Relationship	Status	Age	Occupation	Where born
Thomas Britten	Head	Married	41	Draper	Stoke Bliss
Mary Charlotte Britten	Wife	Married	31		Ingestre
Thomasine Britten	Daughter		4		Birkenhead
Julia Annie Britten	Daughter		2		Birkenhead
Thomas John Britten	Son		1		Birkenhead
Ellen Elizabeth Britten	Daughter		under one month		Birkenhead
Rose Ann Hutt	Assistant	Unmarried	26	Milliner	Stanlake Ox.
Kate Sherring	Assistant	Unmarried	24	Dressmaker	Bristol
Henry Jenks	Assistant	Unmarried	20	Drapers Ass't	Ellesmere
Samuel Platt	Assistant	Unmarried	23	Drapers Ass't	Chester
Elizabeth Proctor	Servant	Unmarried	24	Gen. Servant	Scotland
Martha Madocks	Nurse	Unmarried	29	Nurse	Liverpool

It seems that Thomas Britten our grandfather, his family, shop assistants and servant were all living above the shop.

    My friend Ruth Donnocker from the USA who did the family tree for me says; 'the above was sent to me by a young man I met at the Chester Geneaology meeting. Interesting that the store was called Ginders and Britten. There is a story there, I wish we knew it!'

Index

References to the Britten family are integrated in the text *passim* and so are not included.